HOOP

John Griswold, series editor

Series Advisory Board
Dan Gunn
Pam Houston
Phillip Lopate
Dinty W. Moore
Lia Purpura
Patricia Smith
Ned Stuckey-French

Brian Doyle

HOOP

A BASKETBALL LIFE
IN NINETY-FIVE
ESSAYS

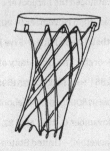

Illustrations by Mary Miller Doyle

The University of Georgia Press

Athens

Paperback edition, 2019

© 2017 by the University of Georgia Press

Athens, Georgia 30602

www.ugapress.org

All rights reserved

Designed by Erin Kirk New

Set in 10 on 15 Sentinel

Most University of Georgia Press titles are
available from popular e-book vendors.

Printed digitally

The Library of Congress has cataloged the hardcover edition of this book as follows:

Names: Doyle, Brian, 1956 November 6–2017 May 27, author.

Title: Hoop : A Basketball Life in Ninety-Five Essays / Brian Doyle.

Description: Athens, Georgia : The University of Georgia Press, [2017]

Identifiers: LCCN 2017014286 | ISBN: 9780820351698 (hardcover: alk. paper) |
ISBN: 9780820351704 (ebook)

Subjects: Doyle, Brian, 1956 November 6–2017 May 27. | Basketball—United States—
Biography. | Basketball—United States—Philosophy.

Classification: LCC GV884.D69 A3 2017 | DDC 796.3230973—dc23 LC record available at
https://lccn.loc.gov/2017014286

Paperback ISBN 978-0-8203-5544-3

For my dear friend
the fine point guard
Bill McAvoy

Harold,
Read at your leisure,
I think you'll enjoy
it as it brought back
memories for me.

Contents

Preface

A few years ago I was moaning to my wry gentle dad that basketball, which seems to me inarguably the most graceful and generous and swift and fluid and ferociously-competitive-without-being-sociopathic of sports, has not produced rafts of good books, like baseball and golf and cricket and surfing have. There *are* good basketball books, like John McPhee's great *A Sense of Where You Are*, and David Halberstam's *The Breaks of the Game*, and Pete Axthelm's *The City Game*, and Bob Ryan and Terry Pluto's *48 Minutes*; and there are weirdly good books, like Terry Pluto's *Loose Balls* and Bill Simmons's maniacal *The Basketball Book*; but where is basketball's Roger Angell, Herbert Warren Wind, C. L. R. James, William Finnegan? Where are the great basketball novels to rival *The Natural* and the glorious Mark Harris baseball quartet and the great Bernard Darwin's golf stories? Where are the annual anthologies of terrific basketball essays? How can a game full of such wit and creativity and magic not spark more great books?

"Why don't *you* write one?" said my dad, who is great at cutting politely to the chase. "Why not you? You're an essayist—write some fine essays poking into every corner of the game you love so, and gather them together, and there you'll have a good book. Anyone who loves the game would enjoy it, and anyone who doesn't know much about the game might enjoy it, and players would enjoy it, if they ever read when they are not playing. Also anyone who *did* play the game would enjoy your book, because they've experienced and remember and miss and love all the things you will have written about, right? So why not you?"

Well, he had a point, and besides, who would argue with my dad, who is the soul of generosity and grace, and also an Army veteran of not one but two wars? Not me. So I wrote it, I hope.

I played basketball two hours a day seven days a week from the age of nine until age thirty-two, at which time I retired (bad back), but I really and truly think that no one ever loved the game more than me. I loved everything about it, the gyms, the playgrounds, the sounds and scents, the camaraderie, the fierce competition, the anticipation and exhaustion, even some of the injuries—nothing was quite so delicious as the thorough soreness in every muscle of your body after playing hard and well the day before—you'd *earned* that sore, you endured it with a strange pleasure, you were *proud* to be sore, you were even, sick man that you are, looking forward to being sore again tomorrow.

So here is a basketball book in which I have tried to remember and report and celebrate everything lovely and sinewy and deeply moving about the game invented one winter day in Massachusetts long ago. I hope, as you read it, that you laugh, and are lured deeper into your own memories of the game; I also hope that you find your sense of the subtleties of the game sharpened a little, ever after; and I suppose I hope that you, too, come to love this sinuous creative swift river of a game a little more than you did. I never tire of watching it, now that I cannot play and do not coach it anymore; but every time I watch a game I see yet another amazing thing—a move, a pass, a feint, an intricate pattern of passes, an extraordinary defensive play, an astounding flurry of shooting—that I never saw before, and I marvel, and am deeply grateful, yet again, to James Naismith, who invented the game as a way to keep his Young Men's Christian Association charges occupied during the long Massachusetts winter. From his inventiveness that December day came great enduring joy for millions of boys and girls and men and women around the world, from the most accomplished stars to little kids in the park picking up a ball for the first time ever. Thank you, Mr. Naismith.

HOOP

HOOP

Tryout

It was a Saturday. I rode my bicycle. I was nine years old. I went alone. It was important to go alone. I brought my basketball. I brought a white shirt, also. My older brother had offered to drive me, but I said no thank you. My mom made me a sandwich to take with me. My dad made toast for breakfast but I could not eat and he didn't say anything. I expected him to say something gently but he didn't. It took me years to see that sometimes not saying anything is way more eloquent than anything you can say. My bicycle was green. My sneakers were white. Colors seemed much more flagrant than usual. The oaks were yellow and the maples were red. I think that every moment you ever lived stays inside you. Tryouts were at nine sharp. Late is not great. Be there early. Be there early to shoot around and look comfortable and catch the coach's eye. Look like you know what you are doing. I was the first boy there. The gym was unlocked. The janitor was finishing the floor with a vast gray broom. It never occurred to me to say thank you to him for that. One light fixture was buzzling. The backboards were tiny and bank shots were out of the question. Stretch before you shoot. Wipe the dust off the bottom of your sneakers regularly. Poor players never do this and they slide like penguins. Never boast or gesture after you score. Act like you expected to score. You don't have to steal the ball; all you have to do is get a hand on it, deflect it, distract the shooter. My older brother had said all this while sitting on the edge of my bed the night before. He wasn't much of a basketball player but he was eight years older and when he said something, it was so. If someone gives you a great pass and you score, just point at the guy casually. Don't say anything. Keep moving. Always be moving.

Never stand still. If you are not getting the ball, just keep running your guy into picks. Set picks as often as you can. Never look at the coach. Let him see you. If you look at him, you are wheedling. If you set picks, he will see you. If you hit the boards, he will see you. If you drive hard to the hole through traffic, he will see you. Grab rebounds with two hands if you can—if not, tip it up again or tip it to a teammate. Just get a hand on it. The coach will see that. Get low when you box out a bigger guy. Hit your free throws. Shoot with your legs. You sure you don't want a ride? Don't wear a headband or wristbands. Bring a white shirt just in case the coach separates guys into two teams. Stay calm. It's just a game in the park on a shinier floor. If you are stuck down low in the lane, don't forget your hook shot. Missing a good shot is better than hitting a bad shot in tryouts. Go right at taller players. They are not as quick as you are. Pretend you are playing against me and, if you score, you get to rag me the rest of the day. When tryouts are over, go and shoot around by yourself for a while at the basket farthest away from the coach. Probably the gym has those stupid dinky tiny butterfly back-boards, so don't shoot bank shots. Hit that little corner jumper from either side like I taught you. You will make the team. That's a lock. Trust me. Just stay calm. Wake me up when you get home. I'd give you a ride but you are right to go by yourself. It's your time. This is the big leagues. Lay out your socks and stuff tonight. Be there early. Bring your ball. Late is not great. Get some sleep. Stay calm. Just pretend all the big guys are me and you are intent on cleaning their clocks and making them look like gawky storks and then do that. Be quick. Stay calm. Keep moving. Every third pick you set, set a half-pick and then roll hard to the basket. Even if your idiot point guard doesn't see you roll, the coach will. OK. No more chatter. Don't eat anything for breakfast. You *will* make this team. Trust me.

First Practice

You stood at the door of the gym with your mom, making sure that this was the correct time and place, and when you were sure, you turned and looked at your mom, and she knew what you meant, and she gracefully withdrew, out of your eyesight; but of course she went to another door and watched you through the window with her heart brimming and tears in her eyes and she was proud and scared and sad and proud; and some of the mothers went to the women's room or to their cars to weep.

You knew one or two of the other kids also trying out for the team, the first organized team, fifth grade, the team you had dreamed about for two years now, and you gravitated toward the kids you knew, but did not make a big deal out of it, because that would be uncool, and also technically you were in competition, so you said hey and maybe touched fists but maybe not, maybe just a glance and hey and then stood near each other, stretching, but not too near, which would be uncool.

You knelt and tightened your laces for the sixth time that morning, and twice you wiped your hands on the bottom of your sneakers for traction, and the coach, who was of course someone's dad, gave a short terse incomprehensible speech, and then Practice began, and you concentrated on making sharp cuts and dribbling with your head up, like your older brother had taught you, and taking only decent shots and not wild silly careless shots, and boxing out in the lane and setting picks and not only trying for rebounds but going up instantly a second time for a rebound when the rebound was unsecured, like your older brother had taught you, because so many rebounds are available the second time, and never getting caught with the ball but making quick firm decisions to get rid of it or jump through a double-team, and twice you made the right quick entry pass into the post, but both times the kid wasn't paying attention, but you didn't say anything or even grimace because you remembered what your older brother had told you about prima donnas.

You did the very best you could not to compare yourself or measure yourself against the other players, or note who was good and who was hapless, or discern who else was playing your position, or glance at the coach to see what he thought when you made a good play or a poor play, or read anything into being placed on one team or another, or being sent in or taken out, because you tried to remember your older brother's advice to just *play*, man, play the way you know you can, a good coach will see what you are doing, you just play right, play generous, play with your eyes open for angles and space, and try to play *some* defense for a change, at least during the first practice, at least make a token *effort* at that end of the floor, and do not always be trying for steals, that is your biggest sin on defense other than not actually *playing* any defense, but that's something we can work on later, for now you just play as hard as you can and use your brains. Don't get rattled. Play quick but calm. You know what I mean.

I did know what he meant, and more than anything in the world I had wanted him to come to this first practice and just stand in the corner so that I could draw some kind of sustenance from him, but he said no, you have to make it or not on your own, man, you don't need me, I would just be a distraction, plus I am busy, and I was hurt and said, OK fine I will make it on my own, *fine*, but at the end of practice, when the coach quietly talked to ten of us one by one and I had made the team and I walked off the court tired and thrilled, there was my brother with our mom, and they were smiling, though you could see that mom had been crying, just a little. She said she had *not* been crying, but you could tell.

The Weave

When I was a boy the first organized basketball team on which you could play was not a team sponsored by a city parks and recreation league, or a team hosted by a for-profit entity, or a team handpicked by men who wanted to sell players to powerful high school programs. No: it was our parish's Catholic Youth Organization team, with its golden jerseys trimmed in liturgical green, and its cheerful gang of coaching dads, and its two practices a week, Wednesday nights in one old echoing dusty wooden gymnasium where the floors were so dusty that you could no-kidding slide easily from the free throw line to the basket, leaving furrows of dust in your wake, and Saturday mornings in a newer gleaming shining burnished wooden gymnasium, where the floors were so meticulously clean and sticky with polish that you would occasionally topple over as your sneakers took root and sent tendrils deep into the strata of the wax.

You had to be in fifth grade before you could try out for the team, and the fifth-grade team had been coached since the Council of Trent by Mr. Torrens, whose idea of offense was the weave, in which the three shortest players among the five on the floor passed to each other for a long while to no effect, way out beyond the foul line, while the defense rested and read beach books, and the two remaining players on offense caught up on the later work of Saint Thomas Aquinas. Our entire first few practices were spent on the weave, until we began to realize slowly that Mr. Torrens did not actually know any other plays, or care much about what we did on the floor, as long as we occasionally ran the weave smartly for him, which we did about once every five minutes, just to perk him up, and because he was the nicest man, always shouting encouragement, though he was not great at names, and called us all Bud. He was the most courteous cheerful man, though, and he was so immediately and patently happy when we ran the weave that sometimes if we were up a few points we would just run the weave for a while on general principle; I don't think the many thousands of fathers who have coached CYO teams in their parishes since the CYO was invented in 1930 have ever properly been thanked, and I am proud to note here that the members of the Saint John Vianney fifth-grade basketball team did their part to thank our coach for his patient service, which was, of course, unremunerated, except in opportunities to see the weave executed beautifully by kids who had practiced the utterly useless maneuver a thousand times, and knew it all too well.

Usually an essay about a basketball team would proceed right here to talk about victories and losses, and dramatic plays, and entertaining exchanges with referees, and the time one of the dads lost his temper and used such foul and vituperative language to a referee that after the game we huddled and wrote down what he'd said so that later we could ask our older brothers what it meant, but this morning I just want to stay with the furrowed dust in the old gym for a moment; and with the parents huddled companionably in the corners of the gym, since there were no chairs or stands or benches for them; and the little brothers and sisters trying hilariously to shoot baskets at halftime, as the referee grinned and shooed them off the floor; and the poor dad assigned to be scorekeeper, who was always falling behind and having to ask who scored last, and the poor dad assigned to be timekeeper, who accidentally blew the horn at the wrong time every single game; and the way when we were up by a few points, a rare and lovely event, we would go into the weave without sign or signal, and then glance over at Mr. Torrens, who would slowly sit up straight as he realized what was happening; and his dawning smile, his open genuine heartfelt glee, was a sight I will always remember, a sight I will always relish and savor and enjoy.

Warm-up

Start slowly and lazily just flipping the ball into the basket with either hand from a couple of feet away to get loose. Then lazy hook shots with your strong hand from five feet away. Then hit at least seven of thirteen hooks from the lane. Do not bother to practice hooks from more than six feet away because you will never shoot a hook from more than six feet away in a game other than in an inconceivable circumstance like a hook from the top of the key to win a game, and if that is the inconceivable position in which you find yourself at the end of a game, the chances of you hitting that are nil, and they will not be improved by practicing such a ridiculous shot. Practice the shots you will actually take in a game so that they are unconscious and easy and normal and your arms and legs and hands are in charge of the shot, with your overactive mind dozing in the back seat. The shot you think about is the shot you will miss.

Then slow lazy layups with your strong hand. Then slow lazy reverse layups with your strong hand. Then a couple of driving layups with your weak hand, on the slight chance that you will be forced into that shot during a game; you want to remind your weak hand of the general concept of shooting, although the cold fact is that if you are forced to drive with your weak hand, you are screwed, and must hope to be fouled, or deliberately angle yourself to get fouled, so that at least it looks like you got hit, rather than that you floated up a wheezing pigeon of a shot. Practice saying *I got hammered!* in case a teammate says *Can you even open a door or comb your hair with your left hand? Does it work at all or is it made of marmalade or what?*

Then jumpers from the left corner. You cannot leave the left corner until you hit ten of thirteen. Then jumpers from the right corner. You cannot leave until you hit ten of thirteen. Then ten set shots from a step deeper in both corners. Remember that this deep in the corner it is your legs that are doing the shooting and your hands are only along as tourists. Then set shots from the top of the key. Then jumpers from either elbow of the lane. Then ten free throws. You cannot leave the line until you hit seven of ten free throws. By right you should hit nine of ten as this is the easiest of all shots but only God and Rick Barry can hit nine of ten.

Then a lap dribbling with your weak hand, then a lap dribbling behind the back, then a lap dribbling between your legs. It will never be the case that you will have more than one instant during a game in which you actually *need* to dribble between your legs but (a) it's fun and (b) it's showy and (c) it gets your hands and the ball and your moving body in synch and (d) see (b). Coaches think showy is bad, and grim efficient point guards think showy is bad, and the sort of guys who are generally named captains of teams think showy is bad, but showy is *not* bad, showy is fun and glorious and entertaining and zestful and deeply satisfying when it works. The only rule that really applies to showy is be as showy as you want but don't screw up or you will hear about it for the next eight hundred years from the sort of guy who thinks that all moves ought to be crisp and effective and efficient and purposeful. If you get into a debate with a guy like that about showiness, you should listen patiently and nod sagely and look him in the eye to indicate that you totally hear what he is saying and it is sensible and reasonable and excellent advice, and then as soon as you possibly can make a double-spin move like Earl Monroe or a blind pass like Pete Maravich just because such loopy creativity is possible and life is short. Listen carefully for the sound of the reasonable guy making a strangled gargle in his throat. Savor that sound. It is a deeply satisfying music, and music, of course, is the greatest of arts.

The Old Gym

Or here's a wonderful redolent crucial part of our Catholic childhoods that we do not talk about much and maybe we should: the sweet spicy sharp stinging scent of the gymnasiums in old Catholic schools, with their slightly sagging stages on which the Christmas pageants were held, and commencement exercises, and the annual visits from His Excellency the Bishop; and the side basketball baskets that folded up to the ceiling if necessary and had to be cranked up and down with a pole a thousand feet long that could only be wielded properly by the gruff wizard of a janitor who knew where everything was and could fix everything and could clean up any and all accidents and could if necessary, like that one time, perform cardiopulmonary resuscitation, not to mention temporarily splint broken fingers and ice swollen ankles, and soothe Mrs. Adams when she wept uncontrollably the day Kennedy was murdered; and the creaking golden dusty wooden floors with their dead spots in the corners toward which seasoned defenders angled their men in crucial moments of games when you needed a turnover in the worst way such as against the powerhouses like Saint Mary Star of the Sea and Saint William the Abbot; and the ancient bathrooms, which probably were imported whole and untouched from the catacombs beneath the Eternal City, and were dotted with heartfelt mosaic messages from the early Christians; and the bleachers, which were folded shrieking and groaning back up against the gym wall by dint of tremendous muscular effort from the whole team even the coach and also as many fathers as could be recruited to push and even that one time Father Pastor although he was older than all the dads put together and rumor had it that he had known Saint Thomas Aquinas personally; and the immense mullioned windows, which also had to be cranked open with long rusty metal poles and which had not been cleaned since the time Elizabeth Taylor borrowed the church for one of her fifty weddings and the church and school and rectory and convent were cleaned and repainted by an anonymous gift from a Welsh actor who married her every five years or so; and the tremendous doors, each heavier than a hill, each reportedly made from metal harvested from Luftwaffe airplanes shot down by members of the parish; and the ancient basketballs, some as flaccid as towels, which shared the utility closet with rubbery dodgeballs and moldy softballs and baseballs stained so green with grass that they looked like fishing floats; and metal folding chairs stamped with the name of the parish and painted a color never seen before and never again in the world except on parish folding chairs, a color something like gray and brown had gotten married and gone to sea for their honeymoon cruise, during which both were terribly seasick; and the occasional sparrow and swallow and even once a crow in the gym, because the kids would prop the emergency exit doors open to ventilate it, knowing that the dramatic signs warning about sirens and alarms were total fiction; and the stray socks and mathematics textbooks and love notes beneath the stage, where you could also find most of the props from the Christmas pageant, not to mention supplies for May Day and unopened boxes of Baltimore Catechisms and most of a bottle of Four Roses whiskey; and the twin basketball baskets, one at each end of the gym floor, one an inch higher than the other, a fact known to the home team, which is why we went that way in the second halves of games; and the baskets' battered backboards, once white but now a sort of pearl gray, with the ghostly imprints of a hundred thousand bad shots stamped faintly on their wood like a code; and the latticed metal struts that proffered the baskets, thirsty for basketballs; and the silvery nylon nets, never whole for more than a day, stitched anew to their stalwart loops before every game by a slight boy sitting on the shoulders of an unsteady burlier boy; and the two referees, aging and slightly paunchy now but sure of their authority and quick to issue technical fouls for abuse of equipment and disrespect of the game; and the squeak and squeal of sneakers during basketball and volleyball and dodgeball and kickball games, the last held in the gym only on days of epic and fearsome and inarguable rain; and here the thought occurs to me that the sweetest sound of my Catholic childhood, perhaps the sweetest song and prayer of all because it was so open and innocent and untrammeled and made by and of and for sheer wild headlong joy, was the music of all those sneakers. Remember?

Your Number

First jersey ever? Basketball, sixth grade, Catholic Youth Organization, number 42, for the legendary Connie Hawkins, who could do whatever he wanted on the basketball court, and score from anywhere, and never seemed to be working hard, but slid easily and sleepily through the freighted air and congested tumult as if he were made of smoke and dreams. That is how I wanted to be but I would never be, though no one else would ever be, either, which is the mark of the finest players, that there is some stamp of idiosyncratic grace and character in their play, and even though you study the parts and pieces of their games, and imitate and ape their maneuvers and logistics, the whole is ridiculously greater than the parts, for reasons that are mysterious and magical.

Next jersey, for two years: number 24, for Bill Bradley, who never stopped moving and cutting and looking for angles and space, and when he found cracks and lapses in the defense, he arose gently from the floor, and drilled a clean unadorned shot that he had practiced a thousand times a day when he was my age, which is why I tried to take a thousand shots a day in the summer, so that I, too, would have a shot so simple and effective and effortless and undramatic that you could watch Bradley for an entire game and think he might have hit five baskets and then discover to your amazement that he had hit ten, and hit all five of his free throws, and made four subtle assists, and once again he had not been the soaring star but a quiet smiling key cog, which is what I wished to be.

Next: number 9, because there were no numbers 42 and 24, and it would be an arrogant fool who would take 10, which belonged to Walt Frazier, or

44, which belonged to Jerry West, or 32, which belonged to Doctor Julius Erving, so I took 9, because it was the only jersey that fit, but told people I had chosen it deliberately to honor Dave Stallworth of the New York Knicks, which was a whopping lie. During the year I wore that number there were people, mostly ebullient burly dads, who would compliment me on wearing Ted Williams's number, or Bobby Hull's number, or Gordie Howe's number, or the atomic number of fluorine (that was Mr. Crouch, who taught chemistry at the high school), or the number of choirs of hierarchical angels according to ancient Catholic tradition (that was Father Driscoll, who knew and loved such arcana), but I never did warm up to the number 9, all due respect to Dave Stallworth, and I switched back to number 42 as soon as possible, which was at the end of the last practice the next year, when the coach dropped a bundle of jerseys on the gleaming court, and guys chose numbers according to seniority, which meant that our terrific point guard chose number 6, for Mike Riordan of the Knicks, and I again reached down, and ruffled through the gleaming green-and-gold jerseys, and pulled up Connie Hawkins.

All the rest of my basketball career, such as it was, I wore that number, and felt at home in it, graceful and alert and creative, sure of myself, protected, watched over or even somehow irreligiously blessed by one of the greatest players ever. I cannot explain very well why certain numbers

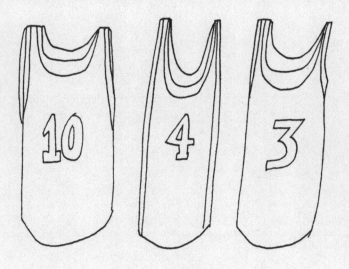

matter to certain people, but I assure you that they do; what number you wear on your back, or on your chest, or stitched on your shorts, does affect your play, and your attitude, and your sense of fit and flow; why this is so is the province of poets or psychologists, I suppose, but rather than try to understand it I would rather simply enjoy the nutty happy silly gentle entertaining arithmetical pleasure of it, and once in a while, on a Saturday afternoon, root through my bureau drawers, and pull out old jerseys, and remember.

Chucks

My first pair of good basketball sneakers meant the world to me, and drew the line between some subtle before and after, and they were lovely, as sneakers go, and my teammates remarked on them with interest, and they lasted that whole first basketball season, and they never inflicted a single blister on me, and I recall them with affection and respect, though I do not have them carefully preserved in a drawer or closet or cedar chest, because that would be weird, and besides at the time of their death they were ragged and redolent, and keeping them would have been a bridge too far, even for me, a total sucker for that which is, in Jorge Luis Borges's great word, *memorious*.

White they were, gleaming and beaming in their original incarnation, though that did not last long, and by the end of the season they were more a gentle yellow or light russet color, having endured rain and snow and slush and sleet and mud and not one but two voyages through the washing machine, which produced the loudest banging noises in the history of the world, as if, said my father, an enraged wolverine were trapped in a tiny office with an insurance adjuster.

Canvas uppers, rubber soles, laces that were far too long and were surreptitiously edited; tongues on which the bearer proudly wrote his last name in tiny indelible letters, so that there would be no doubt on this green and pleasant Earth as to whose shoes they were; the cool and inarguable and immediately recognizable blue star that identified them as Converse Chuck Taylor All Stars; and to wear with them not one but two pairs of serious thick excellent white socks stolen from my oldest brother, who was

15

away in the United States Navy and wouldn't miss them and besides the Navy surely issued socks to its midshipmen and probably our brother was *inundated* by uniform socks far cooler than even these two pairs, which I nicked from his secret stash of good socks, which we younger brothers were *not* to access under *any* circumstances whatsoever, which meant we robbed him blind.

They could not have cost more than twenty bucks, if that. I bought them myself, at a curious store in our town that sold all sorts of sports equipment at once, so that hunting bows and tents and rifles and sneakers and footballs and fishing gear and ping-pong racquets were all exhibited willy-nilly, which now seems to me an eloquent comment on what Americans did for fun at that time in that place. I tried them on in the store and felt bouncy and sinewy and taller. I carried them home under my arm on my bicycle. I forbade my younger brothers to touch them or even look at them too long for fear that their covetous glances would wear out my new sneakers. I hesitated to wear them to practice, but then my father, a reasonable man, pointed out that if I did not break them in during practice they surely would cause me blisters in a game, which would mean fewer game minutes, which would undo the reason that I had paid such a price for such excellent game sneakers, so I did wear them to practice, and continued to feel bouncy and sinewy and taller, and they lasted the whole season, and I loved every minute of that season, primarily because I loved basketball more than anyone who's ever played the game before or since, but also because I had the most excellent sneakers, which I still remember with respect and affection today, as you see.

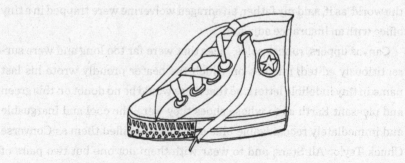

Getting to the Game

In the beginning you would get to the game on your bicycle. The game was on Saturday morning or afternoon and you would ride your bicycle with your gym bag in which was your precious uniform. You would carry your ball just in case the dad who was the coach forgot the game ball, or left it in his car, and his wife took the car to her mother's, or not one but both referees forgot to bring game balls, thinking that the coaches would, but neither coach did, all of which happened, and occasioned the use of the elementary school's ball, which was awful and lumpy and oblong, and the whole game played with that thing was an awful experience too painful to ponder, so you brought your ball, just in case.

Then later when the games were away as well as home you would go in a dad's car, or a mom's car, or the priest's car, or an uncle's car, or a recalcitrant older brother's car, and one time a grandfather's car, which smelled of liniment and onions and pastrami and mustard and gefilte fish and liverwurst and olives and pancetta, because the grandfather ran a delicatessen where sometimes there would be knots of old men speaking all sorts of languages and reading newspapers in other languages and making jokes in other languages and drinking coffee so thick and black it had served in the war and honorably too, as one of the old men told me once.

Then later when it was uncool to go in a mom's car or a dad's car you would go in the bus or the van for winter league, and in a friend's car for summer league, and the friends' cars were always Chargers and Barracudas and Impalas and Mustangs and Falcons, all of which looked cool and sounded cool and thundered satisfactorily, but all of which were incredibly cramped and uncomfortable, especially if you were crammed in with big guys, which you always were, because the center always got the passenger seat for leg room and everyone else folded into the back seat, which was the size of a hatbox and not a very big hat either.

In the last years that I went to games as a player I mostly drove myself, or drove with our immense and hilarious center, but once or twice, in my last season, I rode my bicycle, because the gym was only half a mile away or so, and the car was elsewhere or incapacitated or sulking; and I remember one quiet evening, on the little island where we lived then, riding my bicycle down along the beach, keeping an eye out for chimney swifts and nighthawks, my gym bag swinging from the handlebars, my ball tucked under my elbow, for you should always bring your ball when you go to the game, just in case the other guys forgot theirs, and the janitor isn't there to unearth one of the school's balls, or even if he *does* find one of the school's balls, it's a lumpy oblong pitted rubbery horror that you wouldn't inflict on a church picnic kickball game. Down along the beach and past the harbor; past the buoys and the first fishing boats; under a cathedral of elms, under a startled owl; and finally crunching along the gravel path to the school, where through the open windows I can hear the cheerful rattle and batter of basketballs, as pleasurable and anticipatory and nutritious a sound as I ever heard in this delicious life.

Prelude

Probably my favorite part of playing basketball was not the actual basketball game, but all the hours before and behind the game: practice, which I loved, and drills, which I loved, and rehabilitation after injury, which I loved, perhaps for masochistic reasons. But most of all, best of all, for me, anyway, weirdly, was the prelude to the game—the hour or more we will call, for ease of nomenclature, *warm-ups*.

Let us say that the game begins at seven in the evening, which means that I will be at the gym by five or so, strolling happily into the school, and without fail finding the gym doors locked, and having to track down the custodian, who opens the doors grumpily, and then stomps off muttering about crazy people, but I do not take offense, for he is right about me, as the first thing I do is walk around the court feeling out the floor, and dribbling my basketball in spots that look suspiciously dead, so that I have the geometry and landscape and topography and stratification of the floor in my mind, and can, if necessary, take advantage of that dead spot in the far right corner, and steal a ball if the time comes when we really need a steal.

Then to the bench, or rattling old steel chairs along the sideline, to gird, to meticulously tape my ankles, to properly lace up my sneakers, to carefully stretch; and then the delicious moment in which the ball and I wander out onto the floor to begin the mindless pleasure of warming up. First there is dribbling, the hands and the ball becoming reacquainted; dribbling while walking, dribbling while running, dribbling while spinning, dribbling between the legs and behind the back, dribbling with either hand; and then there is shooting layups, and then short jumpers from the corners and the key, and then short jumpers from the elbows of the key, and then set shots from eight selected favorite spots, and then hook shots, and then a brief fling with shooting left-handed, just in case the occasional desperate chance arises in the game; and then free throws, and then reverse layups, and by now the gym is filling with other players, both my teammates and the opposition, and there is chaffing and greeting, and razzing and teasing, and brief unserious one-on-one tilts, and if we are in a gym with lower baskets on the sides, as so very many elementary school gyms are structured, there is dunking, and laughter.

Finally there are formal warm-ups, which are informal, and usually consist of layup lines and more stretching, and then finally the referees indicate with a nod of their heads that it is time, and the players wander out onto the floor, shaking hands and nodding to acquaintances and friends, and the centers step into the center circle for the initial jump ball, and the game begins; but to be totally honest, I can never remember games that I enjoyed as thoroughly and consistently as I enjoyed all the preludes to the games, which were intent and relaxed at once, and were so often, for me at least, timeless and formless, hours in which the body and the ball and the basket and the dusty gymnasium and the mullioned windows and the squeak of sneakers and the rattle of dribbles and the panting of players were all easy cousins, having nothing to do with loss and victory and conquest and conflict, and everything to do with an energetic unconscious joy. Even now, many years after I had to stop playing basketball, what I miss most is not games, much as I relished them at the time; it is the hours before games, when basketball was loose and free and unaccountable, measured only in units of pleasure.

A Note on Backboards

My first familiarity with the basketball backboard was probably every player's first familiarity with the backboard, which is to say using it as a cushion for your first layups; at age six or eight or so you lined up burbling behind the other burbling guys, and you dribbled awkwardly to the basket, at an oblique angle, trying not to look down at the ball as you dribbled because that's what newbies did, and once in range of the basket, which looked to be eighteen feet high, you endeavored to bank the ball off the backboard and into the unforgiving basket while trying not to trip over your huge sneakers, and trying not to let the ball hit you on the coconut as you stumbled away toward the rebounding line, and all this as your coach or dad or brother or uncle or someone else's dad was barking instructions regarding which leg to jump off, and why we should not aim directly for the basket but use the backboard, and do not stop to shoot but try for one smooth motion, and use one hand not two, and do not attempt cool reverse layups yet, and yes you can go to the bathroom, and other things like that.

Later you tried your first bank shot, which seemed like such an easy cool deft efficient shot when George Gervin or Pete Maravich used it casually in traffic, but you quickly discovered that the shot was devilishly hard, and you had to nail the exact spot on the backboard to bank the ball in smoothly, and this spot was about the size of a quarter, and if you missed, the rebounds caromed and clanged, and you missed so many of your early bank shots that your rebounders came to you in the locker room and said, not politely, that you should either quit shooting bank shots or take hundreds of them a day until you could hit at least half of the things, for they were weary and sore from chasing after the caroms and clangs, and they had a point, you felt, and also they were burly men with short tempers because their legs and bodies were too long and people behind them in movie theaters were always telling them to sit down even though they were already seated.

Then as the years went on you got ever more familiar with backboards of all sorts and types and shapes and construction materials—wooden ones, and metal ones, and glass ones, and butterfly backboards, which we all hated because there was so much less board to use for bank shots, and here and there you would encounter tattered backboards whose wood was shaggy and moist and rotted and probably owls lived in them when no one was playing there, and baskets without backboards at all, and baskets with backboards so incredibly rusted that the ball took on a whole other color by the end of the game, and even once, in Ireland, a backboard apparently, no kidding, made out of turf or peat, which emitted a sad little puffing sound when you banked a ball against it, a sound I had never heard from a backboard before or since.

Even now when I no longer play ball I notice backboards, and admire their sturdy stalwart silent service, and savor their sculptural simplicity, especially the wooden ones; I just saw two the other day that were being given fresh coats of paint by a cheerful young guy who was finishing the square above the basket in green paint against the white of the rest of the backboard. I watched him for a while, smiling at how many boys and girls would soon be aiming for that square as they drove for layups and tried bank shots, and then I proceeded on, happy.

The Grade-School Gym

Most of us who loved basketball and played it every day or twice a day if possible played eventually or regularly in high-school gymnasiums; perhaps your elementary-school or parish team played in the high-school gym in a tournament, perhaps you played on the high-school team, perhaps your rec-league team played its ragged games in the high-school gym; but high-school gyms, in general, are tidy and well-kept places, shiny and gleaming, with good floors and baskets exactly ten feet high and excellent nylon nets, and heat, and locker rooms with showers with actual no-kidding hot water; whereas grade-school gyms are a whole other species of gym, and it is the ramshackle earnest unassuming modest utilitarian grade-school gym that I wish to remember and celebrate this morning.

You remember them, too, I know you do—the floors that were not wood but some sort of hard unforgiving rubber; the floors that *were* wood but clearly milled when Lincoln was a small boy in Kentucky; the ancient thin padding affixed to the walls behind each basket; the utter absence of benches for players, or the battered ancient uneven bench dating from the reign of Tiberius; the scatter of mismatched plastic chairs or folding metal chairs as spindly and croaking as grandfather storks; the nets with gaping holes in them so that when a shot dropped through at a certain angle the referee (almost always a dad with a spit-logged whistle) had to issue a ruling on the spot; the yellowing placards posting inspirational quotations and the rules of the gym; the testy janitor lurking about, disgruntledly waiting for all these interlopers to vacate his beloved floor so that he could lovingly sweep it again with a push broom the size of Idaho; the water fountain that long ago had lost the ability to emit a jet or a spume and now made only a weary aching rusty groaning waterless sound when you leaned on the button; the high windows beribboned with drifting historic spider-strands and small brown stains where moths had melted long ago; the sputter and sizzle of the overhead lights when you turned them on, and the way only two of the three banks of lights awoke, leaving one lane half-lit, as if a whiskey-colored dusk had descended early in that one spot; the way there were always six or twelve light switches on the wall, with no indication as to which switch lit what light; the way the bathroom door was always eternally unforgivingly locked, no matter how many times the coach or the moms or the dads or the league commissioner had requested that restrooms be left unlocked before and during scheduled games and practices . . .

So many of those gyms had a rickety wooden stage at one end of the gym, curtained with huge old thick dusty curtains cut from the weighty sails of clipper ships, and repurposed by a penurious school district with connections to the local seamen's union; and there was that one dusty closet in which could be found balls of every sort and shape and size from red kickballs to green dodgeballs to grassy softballs to sad deflated volleyballs and mangled wiffle balls and lacrosse balls encrusted with mud from the Mesozoic and even somehow for some reason two cricket balls, one white and one red—wouldn't you give anything to know who put two cricket balls in the closet, and why?

Those awful rattling butterfly backboards, imprinted faintly with the reminders of thousands of bank shots; the rims ever so slightly loose, no matter how adamantly the janitor claimed that he'd tightened them; the slush of dust along the sidelines; and always a jacket, a sneaker, a headband, one sock, a lined school notebook, a paperback book that someone had planned to dip into after gym class or before practice while waiting for their kid's game to end; Conrad Richter's *The Light in the Forest*, or Mary O'Hara's *My Friend Flicka*, or John Steinbeck's *The Red Pony*; what an essay might be written about those lost lonely books, and what they said about those who meant to read them, and how the janitor stacked them respectfully in the closet next to those mysterious cricket balls! But this is an essay about grade-school gyms, so here at the end we will flick off the lights (savoring the crackle and fizzle), and check one last time for stuff we left behind, and close the door, and walk home dribbling with one hand for one block and the other for the next.

Mr. Teevan

The best basketball coach I ever had was a brief man named Mr. Teevan. Mr. Teevan might have been five feet tall but he was a brisk brusque amused quick-witted firm-minded man who had graciously accepted the pastor's invitation to coach the seventh-grade parish basketball team of motley lanky cocky shy loud guarded newly teenaged boys. Our intended coach had suddenly vanished and the season opened in a week and Mr. Teevan contacted each boy's parents and explained the situation and scheduled one practice before we faced Saint William the Abbot and Saint Barnabas in a Sunday afternoon doubleheader.

We were all in the gym shooting around and playing pranks when Mr. Teevan walked in. Every one of us was taller than he was, and several of us were a foot taller. None of us had been taller than an adult before, and we were unnerved. Mr. Teevan understood this, I think, and he asked us to sit in a circle at center court. He asked this quietly, but something about the way he said it made it a firm suggestion. Then he delivered a speech that I still think about sometimes when I see old mullioned windows in a gymnasium, or notice a brief brisk man in the street, or hear someone with Mr. Teevan's quick wry amused tone of voice. There was something in his voice that I have heard in a few voices since—a subtle intimation that speaker and listener had no need to pose or preen, that of course we instantly understood each other easily and thoroughly, that certainly the listener knew better than he, the speaker, did about the matter under discussion, but still, it probably ought to be expressed aloud, with a smile, so that we were both clear about what needed to be done, which was, of course, what we, the listeners, already knew needed to be done, and were in fact eager to do, if only he, the speaker, would wrap up swiftly, which he did, and an instant later we were showing him the drills we knew, and walking through the plays we knew, and he was murmuring gentle editing suggestions here and there, which we adopted as soon as he murmured them, and somehow during that practice we unconsciously established a starting team and the first few guys off the bench, doing so without a word from Mr. Teevan, who understood, I think, that players often know players better than coaches do.

I do not remember now if we won many games, but I vividly remember a certain subtle tone to that season, a sort of wry amused brisk brusque approach that served us well. We all played, even the least talented among us, which is not always the case with teams at any level; we all played hard without being commanded to do so; we savored victories and quickly forgot losses; we even practiced hard on our own a few times when Mr. Teevan had to miss practice for something or other. After our last game we asked Mr. Teevan if we could have one last practice, even though there were no more games, and he smiled and said sure, and as he walked into the gym that last night we presented him with a basketball for which we had all chipped in a few dollars each. Mr. Teevan said he was honored at the gift, and while he knew full well the ball was half price, because he had walked past that same store window and seen it on sale, still, to him it was worth ten times the sticker price, because there were ten of us, and he would remember this season the rest of his life. Then we had a great loose practice, which ended with Mr. Teevan shooting free throws with us, and then he shook our hands and left the gym as briskly as he had entered it the week before the season opened.

To the Dads and Moms
Who Coached Catholic Youth Organization
Teams in Every Conceivable Sport

Gentlemen and ladies: I wanted to say thank you. The pastor may or may not have managed to express his gratitude, as he is crazy busy with confessions after the election; and the diocesan sports director *feels* gratitude, although she is still bitter about the whole lacrosse incident, during which candlesticks were brandished, which is *not* what candlesticks are for; and the parents and grandparents of the children you coached feel gratitude, even if you did not play Humphrey and Mustafa and Rainbow and LaMaKeysha quite as much as you could and *should* have played them, if you had *any* eye for talent; but I will step into the breach here and say thank you for volunteering (albeit reluctantly), and showing up every single time for practice (despite that amazing fact that the Seattle Mariners were finally in the World Series), and making every single game, not only the home games but the ones in Alfalfa, Cornucopia, Donnybrook, Fossil, Horse Heaven, Idiotville, Mohawk, Owyhee, Pistol River, Rufus, Ruggs, Wolf Creek, Wonder, and Wren.

All those practices during which your young charges had belching contests instead of stretching properly during warm-ups. All those hours of driving Matty and Billy and Jenny and Jessie home after practice because the older sister who was supposed to pick them up got lost in the shallow electric wilderness of her phone. The way you quietly bought the jerseys yourself before the first game because the system for reimbursement is clogged and the kids needed the jerseys and it would be just wrong to not have a clean fresh new jersey before your first game, and also the happy chaos and hubbub of picking jersey numbers is one of the funniest things in this wild world. The way your wife and kids chipped in again and again without fuss or fidget or comment or complaint, driving and cooking and juggling family time and duties and shelling out majorly for the end-of-the-season picnic. The way you tried endlessly to show the kids that there is joy in playing a game well, and joy in the camaraderie of teammates, and joy in fervid competition, and dignity in treating the referees and umpires and scorekeepers and other team's players with integrity and respect, and something very much like prayer in the vibrant vigorous creative imaginative diligent delighted use of the holy vessel that the Creator gave you as a body. There is something deeply reverent in hard work, and focused act, and sharing the ball, and not quitting, and in playing hard right to the end, even though you are down by thirty, and the other team appears to be comprised of ten girls who are all going to Notre Dame together directly from eighth grade, bypassing the usual admissions regulations because they are that good.

It may well be the case that you became the coach only because all the other dads backed out, or because the college kid who was going to be the coach suddenly decided to enter a monastery in Ecuador, or because you lost a bet to the pastor on the Mariners game, but the fact is that you did become the coach, and did work awfully hard to teach the kids the rudiments of the game and something of the subtle pleasures and delights of it, and they will remember your generosity all their lives, in some deep secret chambers of their hearts, and maybe the final assessment of how well you coached will be the fact that almost all of them someday will volunteer themselves, albeit reluctantly, to coach their parish teams. That will be the best thanks you ever get, and you will not get it, not directly; but I thank you directly, right here, right now, for your grace, your generosity, and those glowing new jerseys. Gentlemen and ladies, well done.

In a Schoolyard in New York

Two of the most remarkable things I ever saw on a basketball court arrived together without warning one summer afternoon in a schoolyard in New York. The court was ancient pitted asphalt with rafts and herds and shards of pebbles of all different shapes and colors, so many that sometimes you wondered if the asphalt was decaying even as you played on it, and if the court was ever so slightly sinking back down to bedrock, and soon you would be playing basketball in a hole so deep you would never come out, and never go to college, or get a decent car, or maybe someday even be granted a girlfriend, if God was gracious and overlooked your more egregious sins, like letting that guy cut backdoor for easy baskets on you not once but *twice* in the first half, man, *stop* looking at the ball and keep one eye on your man, or one hand on his shirt if necessary, just do *not* let that happen again, OK? OK?

We were playing three on three full court, the most perfect of all permutations of the game, for it opens up the play, and rewards sprinting and sharp passing, even as it still allows for picks and screens and such; but while four of us were decent ballplayers, two of us were *very* good players who would go on to play college ball. Neither of these guys was physically prepossessing, neither was particularly tall or brawny or jumpacious, but both were quick as cougars, and masters of the unexpected spin, the stutter step, the pump fake, the look-away pass; both, in short, loved the intricate chess of the game, and understood how the slightest flicker of movement could shift a defender out of the way; and both, too, were gifted passers who *liked* to pass, relished the zest of a terrific pass, savored the florid theater of the improbable pass. Also neither of them was ever out of position, both of them were excellent shooters, and they'd been friends since kindergarten. So, because they were friends, they were twice as intent on beating each other every time out; and that is what they'd set their minds to do this afternoon.

Because both of them were generous by nature, they spent most of the game feeding their teammates, and setting us up for easy buckets, and working the boards themselves dutifully, and only taking good shots, and not taking over for searing incendiary scoring runs, though both could very easily have done so; indeed I had seen them each do so many times in our games in that pebbled schoolyard, where I had watched both of them mature suddenly from good to great; a mixed pleasure, that, because both of them were suddenly much better than me, and I was older, at a time in life when a young man is very jealous indeed of the privileges of his seniority. But another thing to love about basketball is that you cannot argue with it; when one guy is better than another, he is just better, and that's that, and you can either whimper about it or learn to enjoy it.

The game was close all the way to the end, and then the very good players, with the tacit agreement of their teammates, took over the controls, and they went basket for basket for a few minutes, each basket more impressive than the last—twisting amazing drives, impossibly long jumpers, a hook with the wrong hand, even once a basket on a shot in which the shooter just tossed it in unconcernedly over his shoulder as he floated past the basket facing in the wrong direction; I had never seen a basket like that before, and interestingly have never seen it again, though I have watched many thousands of games since that afternoon.

In the last minute of the game I was driving down the sideline and lost the ball, and the very good player on my team, running behind me, lunged for it as it started to sail out of bounds toward the rectory; but by evil chance he slipped on a scrabble of pebbles and wrenched his ankle as he jumped for the ball. By then I had spun around to grab for it also, and I think I will always remember his face; it was twisted in pain, and also, I think, with that awful knowledge of the extent of your injury that you develop as a basketball player; when you have sprained your ankle twenty times, you know, the instant it happens again, how screwed you are, and how fast it will balloon, and what colors it will turn, and how long you will be sidelined; I know it sounds fanciful, but I thought I saw all that in his face as he hung there in the air out of bounds.

But then the first remarkable thing happened. Had it been me who had just wrenched an ankle, I would have fallen in a heap cursing like a deacon, and probably hurt my hand slamming it in frustration on the asphalt. But my friend the very good ballplayer, while hanging in the air, grabbed the ball, and somehow, through some combination of vision and anticipation it was never my grace to share, snapped the ball right to a teammate under the basket for an easy score.

I helped him up and he limped back onto the court. He knew and we knew that this was a bad sprain, and he ought to get home right now and ice it, if he was going to have a prayer of not being out for a week, but the game was now tied, and without anyone saying anything we all agreed that the next basket wins.

The other team got a good shot—their very good player fed a guy for an open jumper, which he missed, but it was the right guy and the right shot— and I got the rebound. By instinct I looked up and saw our very good guy already out on the break, and I whipped it to him as hard as I could; but he was really hobbling, and even as he got close to laying in the winning basket we could see the other very good guy bearing down on him like a hawk.

But then the other remarkable thing happened. I still think about it sometimes, and I always find myself smiling about it, because it didn't make sense, which I have come to appreciate more and more over the years, how sometimes the coolest things of all are the ones that don't make sense. Our very good guy, quite aware of his friend bearing down on him, suddenly stopped and tossed the ball up over the basket, and the other very good guy, somehow understanding this gesture, jumped as high as he could, caught the ball, and dunked it. He hung on the rim for a second, smiling, and then hopped down, and he and his friend touched fists, and so we won by a basket, even though we had not scored.

What Was the Worst Gym
You Ever Played In?

A basketball-mad son asks me what was the worst gym I ever played in, and instantly a parade, a procession, a panoply of ratty sagging dusty icy dim bandbox gyms come to mind, one after another, leering at me from the far-away past, for those gyms actively strove to stop you from dribbling and shooting, with their endless dead spots in the floor, and their baskets of any height at all except the regulation ten feet, and their rattling paint-flaked backboards where no kidding you could see the bolts worming their way out of the wood with every carom, and their medieval mullioned windows that refused to let in light even in the full blast of summer, and their mere inches between the non-bleacher sideline and the brick wall and the baselines and the brick wall; but one gymnasium in particular came clearest to mind, for this was the dustiest gym that ever was, and I will tell you of this gym, so that you too can gawp at a gym so dense with dust that you could, as I can attest, slide through the dust leaving long runnels behind you and contrails raised by your passage.

I kid you not. This was at Saint William the Abbot Catholic Church in Seaford, New York, on the south shore of old Walt Whitman's fish-shaped isle of Paumanok. Our parish basketball team played their parish basketball team there twice a year, and the legends of the gym at Saint William were handed down from one year's players to another: how a player from our parish had been lost once in a dust drift, and not found until two days later during a school assembly announcing that the Holy Ghost was henceforth to be called the Holy Spirit; how a player from their team, after three games in two days during a holiday tournament, inhaled so much dust that his chest expanded noticeably and his father had to go buy him a large bra; how a referee who had never seen the gym before got there early to stretch, and entered alone, and was found in a trance by his partner referee, who subsequently reffed the game alone; how a janitor had once attacked the gym with a vacuum cleaner, then a broom and a mop, and had to go on short-term disability soon thereafter, costing the parish a pretty penny; and how an exorcist had once been called, to no avail, although he worked so hard he fainted and required whiskey.

Part of the reason for the dust in Saint William's gym, I think, was that it wasn't really a gym, but an auditorium with baskets mounted at either end; the floor was linoleum, and God help the poor boy who dove on or crumpled to or was knocked to that adamant floor; you felt it for weeks afterward. And Mass was held there in the mornings, so that when we slid onto the floor in a basketball game, we were sliding through the leavings of hundreds of shoes, and shards and scraps of church bulletins, and coins, and hairpins, and lost rosary beads, and crumbles of crackers, and the occasional hat or scarf or glove, and even once, amazingly, a tiny pile of Communion hosts, like a prayer cairn, right under the basket, perhaps left by a mournful center after a particularly tough afternoon in the lane.

I cannot remember now if we won or lost games in that gym; besides the dust, the other aspect I remember most is how a tall wooden stage formed one sideline, so that you could, if the referee wasn't looking closely, whip a pass off the stage wall to a teammate behind your defender, as if you were playing epic billiards. I have a vague memory of Saint William players constantly wiping the soles of their sneakers with their hands and towels, but that may have been some religious observance having to do with their saint, who was so austere a leader of men that he was thrown out of the monastery he'd founded. Mostly what I remember are things like fast breaks during which players floated as if they were on skates, and leaving actual no-kidding footprints in the dust when you ran, and taking two showers when you got home, even though your sister was pounding on the door and using the most vulgar and shocking language.

A Note on Dribbling

One summer I decided to learn to dribble my basketball with my left hand while riding my bicycle slowly along flattish streets. This was the apex of my adventures in dribbling, which included a month spent dribbling with only my left hand, and a month spent dribbling behind my back with my right hand for a day and my left hand for a day, with occasional days spent dribbling mostly between my legs, and other days spent dribbling between and among chairs and bicycles and brothers set up as obstacle courses. I was intent on being a decent dribbler and one virtue I had then, among very few others, was a ferocious concentration on the smallest of things, things that usually other people thought peculiar or insane, like learning to dribble with your left hand while riding a bicycle along flattish surfaces.

I rode down every level street I could find in our neighborhood. I rode through and around every parking lot of every grocery store, often arranging the loose shopping carts as an obstacle course. The cart shepherd at Waldbaum's did not mind this, but the cart shepherd at the Great Atlantic and Pacific Tea Company store minded exceedingly, and would chase after me using vile and vituperative language. I would ride through church lots and temple lots and the Lutheran church lot, which was small and narrow which made me wonder about the Lutherans. I tried riding through the streets in the new developments south of the highway in our town, but it turned out the new developments had their own security guy who for some reason disliked the thump of basketballs early in the morning, and he chased me so assiduously in his Pinto that I decided to avoid those particular streets.

My father, a wry and sensible man, observed me one day riding along our street while dribbling with my left hand, and he noted later that he was not aware of times during basketball games when dribbling left-handed while riding a bicycle was a useful skill, except perhaps as halftime entertainment, but I pointed out that all dribbling practice was good practice, which was why, for example, I had spent another recent summer with cardboard taped over the lower half of my spectacles, so I could not look down at the ball while dribbling, which is a common sin in dribbling, and my father said he remembered that summer all too well, son, all too well, so that if I wanted to spend *this* summer dribbling while riding a bicycle or a goat, that was fine by him, although I was on my own regarding the goat. *He* was not in the goat business, he said, although there are a number of goats in this town, but it would not do to pursue this line of talk further, or he would be guilty of calumny.

By the end of August I was actually pretty good at dribbling left-handed while riding my bicycle, and when basketball practice began that autumn our coach noticed that I was lot more sure with the ball with my off hand, and he asked me what I had done during the summer to repair what had been a noticeable hole in my game, and I told him about dribbling while riding a bicycle. I explained about which parking lots and streets were better than others, for example that the Lutheran's were narrow, and he listened carefully and courteously and then he gestured and told his assistant coach to take over practice, and then he went outside, I think to clear his throat from all his cigar smoking, because he made a choking sound we could hear through the open windows of the gym, and when he came back inside a few minutes later he was wiping his eyes. At the end of practice, I remember, he added a new drill in which each guy had to dribble the length of the court five times with his off hand—a drill, he said, inspired by something he had heard recently that interested him very much indeed, boys, very much indeed.

Rims and Nets and Courts

A Note

There were bent rims and double rims and loose rims and rims so tight that after you missed your first few shots you concluded privately that not even Jesus could score at this bucket and He had major serious hops.

There were rims that were higher on one side than on the other, so that a jumper from one side was as easy as dropping a ball in a hole, but a jumper from the other side was inarguably impossible, although that didn't stop certain arrogant souls from trying.

There were rims that were weirdly tipped up at the front, as if the rim were defending itself, which forced you to use the backboard even on jumpers from straightaway, which was unnerving, and made you feel like a goober shooting the first jump shot of your life.

There were rims that were an inch low and two inches low and even once five inches low, a rim in Queens I remember well because no one could calibrate his shots on that peculiar thing for the first ten minutes, and rarely do two teams of decent players go for ten minutes without a single basket being scored, but with beautiful and creative cursing, I remember that.

There were rims that hung by a single fragile strut so that every time the ball went through you thought this was the end of the rim altogether and thought that the thing would crash down on some unsuspecting center's head, not that a center would even notice such a light and glancing blow.

And then there were the nets—steel nets, cord nets, no nets, rusted nets, nets half-attached, half nets, metallic mesh nets in which the links had become tangled so that when a shot went in the ball got stuck and someone would have to jump up and pop the ball back out. But all nets, even the worst nets, were better than no nets, because no nets meant arguments all game long as to whether or not the ball had actually gone through or not; it was on courts with no nets that I began to realize that the guys who argued most assiduously about shots going in or not, and fouls being committed or not, and guys stepping out of bounds or not, were never the best players, and that as a rule the better the player the less he said on the court, a rule that seems to me now to apply generally to the wider world, in which the greater the accomplishment the less he or she who accomplishes it needs to chatter about it, whereas the reverse is true, that the lesser the accomplishment the more excuses and blather and lies and sales pitches there are.

Ponder *that* for a while.

Finally, regarding the courts themselves, a splendid array of possible courts, from oak to pine to maple to concrete to cement to asphalt to rubber to dirt to packed sand to mysterious plastic substances in every imaginable color. In the matter of the material of basketball courts, there is no end to what the imagination can produce and inflict on the whimpering knees of players; yet we played on them, thrilled to be playing on a court at all, even as the ball inevitably found dead spots and ridges and pits, and you slid for yards at a time on pebbled glass or sand, and the ball gathered unto itself every scrap of silt and dot of dust, so that by the end of the game your hands were grimy, and your sneakers were a shade darker than they had been that morning; but at least the rims were decent, and there was blessedly a net at one end, and the ball was not oblong and lumpy, and the players were decent and cheerful and intent, and the game had revealed itself once again to be quick and swift and generous, rewarding creativity and confidence, but punishing arrogance and selfishness; and so we went home, tired but happy, and thinking maybe we could get one more game in tonight before the park guys turned the lights off at ten o'clock, with that familiar pop and sigh and sizzle.

Boxing Out

A Note

I am that rare man who can vividly remember his first lesson in the dark art of boxing out other players under the basket, a workmanlike task necessary before you or a teammate could snare a rebound. It was a warm Saturday morning, many years ago, in a grade-school gymnasium, and our coach, one of the other guys' dads, was animatedly showing us how the proper technique is to position yourself between the opponent and the basket, and crowd up against your opponent close enough that you are sure he is stuck or rooted there behind you, and then you spread out your arms widely but innocently, without smacking anyone in the kisser, and cocking your elbows slightly as warnings against incursion or trespass into the space you thus create in which you or a teammate can snare the rebound, then, the most important part, boys, the crucial part, the secret of the thing, is that you *crouch down low,* as if you are about to sit down awkwardly on the pot, and you hold that position as long as necessary, and the genius of this crouch, boys, is that your posterior acts as a lever to further establish your secure position against the incursion or trespass of the fella who is stuck there behind you, and also it creates a little more space over which bigger fellas have to reach over you for the rebound, and referees *hate* it when guys reach over other guys, even the *appearance* of reaching over another guy for a rebound is enough to make the refs blow their whistles, which they love to do, I think to prove that they exist on this God's Earth, and are in charge of the game, and can blow their damned whistles, although how hard is it to blow a whistle, hey? OK, you guys try to box me out.

And for the next fifteen minutes there was the hilarious uproarious vastly entertaining sight of a parade of scrawny eleven-year-old boys trying manfully to box out our coach, who was a tall eager cheerful man with the face of a disconsolate bulldog and not the slightest hint or shred of athletic ability. We took turns jumping in front of him, opening our dewy wings wide, crooking them slightly so as to emphasize our pencil-point elbows, and then crouching and *owning* our position, that's *your* spot, boys, no force on this God's *Earth* can dislodge you from your spot, you are *camped out* there, and that ball is *yours*, it has your *name* on it, or your teammate's name, and the only way your opponent can possibly get to it is *through* you, and that won't happen, will it, boys? Or he can try to reach over you, and the referee will blow his whistle if that happens, in fact he will blow that damned whistle if your opponent even looks like he is *thinking* about reaching over you, trust me on this one, boys, trust me.

He was a most pleasant and energetic man, our coach, the kind of guy who actually bounded from place to place in the gym, though he had not the slightest scrap or speck of athletic ability, so that it was like watching a clunky rabbit lurching joyously from place to place; I don't think I ever saw a happier coach in my life, although the only play he knew was the weave, which is a silly and pointless play, though fun to watch if you enjoy journeys with no particular destination in mind.

In the twenty years I played basketball after that morning I learned many other entertaining things about boxing out, such as how to back up steadily while you are crouched and so take away the legs of taller players, and how to pretend you have been shoved out of position when you haven't, and how to accidentally elbow your opponent sharply in the throat while establishing position, and how to shove a guy who has established position off the spot you want, and how to hold a guy's shirt with both hands and yank down when he tries to jump so that he can't, and how to box out a guy by just flashing in front of him at the right instant, and how to box out huge guys by accidentally getting all tangled up with them for an instant while your teammate floats by and snares the rebound, and many other subtle and satisfying things like that, but even now when I hear the words *boxing out* I think immediately of that bright Saturday morning many years ago in a grade-school gymnasium, as we learned to hold our position against all sorties and assaults, boys, against all trespass and incursion, against the devious plots and wiles of the opposition, not to mention the referees, never put your faith in the referees, boys, for they are not above blowing their whistles occasionally just to assure themselves that they are still alive. They are not the brightest bulbs in the universe, boys, and that's a fact. Trust me on this one.

Boarding School

My master tutor in the bruising craft of rebounding was the first good center I played with, a long lean gruff terse seemingly grumpy guy who was actually gentle and funny and shy off the court, despite his fearsome visage and eternal stubble; he was the kind of guy who had started to shave in kindergarten, and had a five-o'clock shadow five seconds after he shaved. He was well over six feet tall, and thin, but one of those thin guys who seem to be made of steel wire; he was lot stronger than he looked, as opposing centers discovered from the first moment they jockeyed with him in the lane.

It was Bobby who taught me that rebounding was mostly a matter of space and *want*; as he said, most rebounds are taken below the rim, many rebounds go to the guy who just wants them the most, and leaping ability is vastly overrated. He had little respect for leapers, and much enjoyed shoving them away from the basket just as they launched, so that they would soar out of view like gulls retreating from a garbage scow after a thorough looting of its savories.

No, he said, rebounding is not about leaping, and it's not even all about boxing out, although that's important. It's about carving out space, and any idiot can do that, even you, if you put your mind to it, for once, and stop lollygagging around out there in the perimeter, barking and embarrassingly waving for the ball, and hoisting foolish shots as soon as you do get the ball. No, no—come in down in the lane with me and I will show you how to work. Even *you* could grab eight boards a game with a little effort. That's a compliment, you know—most guards and a startling number of forwards are the most hapless lazy useless rebounders imaginable, so bad at it that when they have the occasional silly urge to come down here I send them out again right quick for their safety and my sanity.

The first rule of rebounding, said Bobby, is to get your spot and hold it. Then you *expand* your space, sort of—see what I mean? You spread out, using your legs and arms; never use your hands in ways the referee can see. That's all they look for, refs, you know, hands and the ball. Mostly the ball. They are like little children gaping at the big bright shine. But they'll blow the whistle instantly if they see your hands at work. They hate hands. Who knows why? Anyway, then you gauge the flight of the ball. A missed shot from in close will probably trickle off the rim, whereas a missed shot from far away will probably ricochet. A missed jumper from the corner is usually long, and will rebound toward the other corner. The higher the arc of the shot the more likely it is to go in, but when it misses it will bounce pretty high. Yes, I watch the other team warm up, but that's not to get a sense of how they miss as much as it is to see which hand they shoot with, and where they are comfortable. When guys get tired their shots start to fall short and you take that into consideration when rebounding. If there's a terrific rebounder on the other team and I can't outwork him, I try to seal him off so that *you* guys can get the boards. Remember that game that you hauled down seven rebounds and thought you were so cool and brawny? I sealed off their one decent rebounder for you, you dolt, and did I get a thanks from you? I did not. It's OK. Let it go. All I worry about is forwards and centers; it's a rare guard who even bothers to follow his shot, let alone slash down the lane for a rebound. Mostly they are out there admiring their form and wondering if their hair looks good. Last thing to remember is to grab the thing with authority. Use two hands if you can, one if possible, and if you can't grab it, tip it to me. If you can get one hand on a rebound, and the ref is right there, stagger as you grab it, and he'll call a foul on the other guy. Referees are pattern monkeys and anything that breaks the pattern sets off their whistle reflex. Never say anything, though. Never complain or grunt even when you do get hammered. They'll give you two or three free fouls per game if you don't say anything. Believe me I know what I am talking about here.

Which he did; he was a ferocious rebounder, tireless and relentless and, I think, delighted to outwork and outthink opposing centers and forwards.

He was the first, and for a long while the only, guy I ever played with who really didn't care much about his points, but he cared very much about his rebounds, and he did regularly check the scoresheet after a game to see how many he had been credited with—always one less than he thought he had, a phenomenon he called, grumpily, the keeper margin of error. But it didn't bother him overmuch. As he said to me after one bruising game, *he* knew what had been going on all night long in the mosh pit of the lane, even if no one else did, and anyway fifteen rebounds was a very good night's work, whether or not it was actually sixteen, but who's counting?

A Basketball Story

It's a little story, I suppose, and it happened a long time ago, but it keeps coming back to me, and every time it surfaces again from the pool of memory I find myself staring at it from a different angle. This fascinates me: could it be that all memories are alive and active and changeable, and they live vibrant mysterious lives in the depths of your flickering memory, and they are like other people's children, who are new beings every time you see them again at wakes and weddings and parole hearings?

So then. We are on a basketball court in New York. It is summer. The court is near enough to the Atlantic Ocean that you can smell low tide, and gulls and herons drift over, and in the winter if you stop by the court to get in an hour of shooting you sometimes slide on a scatter of sand. It's just dusk; the light-towers are hissing awake. It's the first game of a summer league doubleheader. It's a good league; some of these guys will go on to play college ball. We have a decent team but not a fine one because we are in the league for fun. We like to run and gun and try to dunk and we don't mind losing by ten. We dislike losing by more than ten and if we fall behind by more than ten we go to our best player, who hauls us back by himself. He is the most unprepossessing good player you ever saw. He has zits, and his hair is a mess, and he has geeky eyeglasses held onto his head with a black elastic band. He is a gawky guy without any discernible muscles but he is a stunning leaper and he is a deft and efficient scorer when he wants to be. He rarely wants to be. He loves rebounding and that is mostly what he does if we do not call upon him to be a deft and efficient scorer for a while. He wears ragged low-cut black sneakers that he inherited from an older brother. He is the palest person we know, even after a summer playing ball in the sun and going to the beach to ogle girls. He mostly wears a goofy smile. He is an affable soul except about his car. You do not mess with his car. We drive to games in his car. There is no eating or drinking in his car. There are no wet towels or wet shorts in his car. You do not take off your sweaty sneakers and socks in his car. These are the rules and if you observe the rules he is an affable guy.

Tonight we are playing a team we do not know. The ref tells us they are from the town where Julius Erving was born. Their center glowers at us when we come out for the opening tip. Our best player jumps center for us because he can jump to the moon. He wins the tip and we run our standard opening play, which produces a baby hook for him that he never misses. My theory is that he never misses because he is shooting down rather than up like the rest of us. This time he rolls into the lane for his baby hook and just as he lets it go the other team's center smashes him in the face. It sure looks to me like a deliberate foul but the ref doesn't call it. This is summer league and the ref may or may not be sober.

Our man shakes off the foul and we drift back on defense. The other team works the ball to their center and he goes up for a hook also and as he shoots with his right hand his left arm swings out and smashes our man in the face. It sure looks to me like a deliberate foul again but again the ref doesn't call anything.

We walk the ball up, waiting for our man to adjust his eyeglasses, which have been knocked awry, and without anything being said we run the same play to get him the ball again so he can score on this horse's ass of an opposing center, and amazingly the same thing happens, our man hits his lovely baby hook and gets smashed right in the face so hard we can all hear the smack, and this time we bark at the ref, who snarls back and doesn't call anything, and we drift back on defense, annoyed.

But some little thing has changed, and this is the memory that comes back to me every few months or so. Sometimes I remember this moment and I see the light stanchions casting their huge webs of brilliance on the empty softball fields adjacent to the basketball court. Sometimes I see all the guys who were on the court with me that evening. Sometimes I hear the last gulls and the first owls. Sometimes I smell the asphalt and salt and sweat and the marinating marsh beyond the floodlights. Sometimes I see the boy I was, shy and sinewy.

The other team goes to their center again, and he rolls across the lane for a hook, and our man catches his shot and throws it right into the guy's face, as hard as he can. It is a clean block and the ref couldn't possibly call a foul, so he doesn't, but the other team's center is furious, and he spends the rest of the game shoving and banging and elbowing our man, but I am here to tell you, without the slightest exaggeration or hyperbole or fiction, that the other team's center does not score the rest of the game. Every single time he shoots the ball it is blocked by our best player, who has a grim ferocious look we have never seen before except in regard to his car.

Early in the fourth quarter the other team's center makes a sudden smart play and steals a lazy pass from me to our point guard. This is at midcourt, where you do not expect a big guy to be lurking, nor do you expect him to be quick enough to steal a lazy pass, but steal it he does, and since we are up by about twenty points at the time both of us guards just lazily let him go, thinking that the poor arrogant lump will finally get an easy basket and feel better about himself after being humiliated by the geekiest good player ever, plus it is summer league and who cares and there's no glaring coach pacing the sideline ready to lecture us about relentless perseverance and consistent effort and character-building and other such nonsense.

But as the other team's center cruises in for his easy basket our best player shoots past us and takes off and pins the guy's shot to the metal backboard so hard that the backboard shivers and there is a sort of dark baritone ringing sound.

I have no idea how many shots our man blocked that night, or how many points he scored, or even how many points *I* scored. I remember a lot of things about that evening, like the fizzling lights, and our man peering at his black elastic strap as he tried to get his eyeglasses back into place, and the way the rest of us glanced at each other as we realized we were seeing something amazing, but oddly it is the sound of that ball being slammed against the backboard that I think I will remember best. It wasn't the sound of a bell or anything like that—the old backboard was steel with holes drilled in it, you know the kind I mean—but it was a remarkable sound. It was a real firm and inarguable sound. I don't think I ever heard that sound again, and even if I did hear the exact same sound now, it wouldn't mean what it meant the first time I heard it, on a basketball court in New York, in summer, long ago.

On the Outdoor Basketball Court
at the Syracuse University Married Housing
Apartment Complex

Even though my cool gruff amused tall broad witty wry older brother has been dead for two years, I think about him all the time, and every time I think of him I remember another story, and I have the powerful urge to call him up and hear his gruff terse *Hello?*, which always sounded just like a suspicious walrus would sound, and I want to tell him the story I just remembered, and then with deep pleasure listen to his quiet laughter, which sounded like a washing machine in the basement, or a battered old window fan upstairs.

The story I just remembered was a cold windy day on a ratty basketball court not far from the Canadian border. The court was a mess but we were intent and I had not seen him for a while and I was still very much the younger brother and he was the oldest and smartest and biggest and I loved him and was afraid of him. We warmed up and I noticed that moves and shots that came easily to me were laborious for him. It wasn't that he was old—he was a grad student and I was seventeen—but for the first time I realized he was not a natural basketball player. He was a hard worker, the kind of big guy who banged the boards relentlessly, and set massive picks, and was always in the right place, but he wasn't quick and easy about any of this. He had to *work*, where for me it was delicious play. I am not talking about talent, or athleticism; more like a subtle but telling difference in our games. For me basketball was water and laughter and something I loved to do more than anything else in the world; for him it was a fun pastime, a workout, something he enjoyed but did not do easily and joyously, the way he did, for example, mathematics, at which he was beyond brilliant.

Another way to say this, perhaps, is that mathematics was his natural language, and basketball was mine.

And I seized this epiphany with evil joy, sure I did, and I zipped everywhere that day, thrilled to discover I was better at something that he was! For the first time ever! I couldn't believe it! And yes, I beat him, one game and then two, and I said *We done?* And he said *One more*, and I beat him a third time, reader, yes I did, and I savored every blessed second of the sweep, sure I did; but that's not the story. This is.

Near the end of the third game, he took the ball, and turned around, and backed down slowly to the basket, dribbling metronomically, inch by inch, until he got close enough to toss in his awkward but effective hook shot. Score. Then he did it again. Score. And again. Score. I remember the little dirty rills of snow along the edges of the court, and the fat rectangle of sweat like a dark door on his shirt, and the cutting wind. He was tired and I was exhausted from trying to keep him from the basket and he outweighed me by fifty pounds and he turned and backed in again, inch by inch, while I tried with all my might to hold my ground, but down the lane he came, irresistible and inevitable, until he was close enough to toss up that little awkward hook shot; but now he was weary, and he missed, and I grabbed the rebound and whirled away, relieved to finally be out of his shadow.

But here's the story: he and I looked at each other, and he smiled the smallest subtlest blink-and-you-missed-it smile ever. That's what I wanted to tell you, him bent over dripping with sweat and looking at me and smiling a little tiny smile that wasn't at all about passing the torch or any of that stuff but all about respect and affection and amusement and love. That's what I wanted to tell you. Just that. The small smile that wasn't small at all. It was as big as he was. Still is.

Rules of the Game

If there is a game going, and you want to play the next game, you cannot just murmur *Winners*. You must wait in the corner of the court for a break in the action, and then loudly say *Hey, we got next, OK?*, and your clear claim must be acknowledged by at least two players on the court. *Quod lucutus est verus*; that which is spoken is real.

If there is more than one claimant to the next game, you must sit or stand in a prominent position along the baseline or the sideline, and incarnate the primacy of your claim. You cannot call *Next!*, and be acknowledged as such, and then go lie in the grass and expect a messenger to come inform you respectfully that sir, your time has come. If your claim is not represented corporeally, there is no claim. *Et quod corpus sit indicio*; the body is the evidence.

When choosing from among unknown players to compose your team, do not automatically choose the tallest or broadest guy; throw him the ball first, to see if he catches it with his face, and see if he can run up and down safely, or if he is, like so many big guys, a large houseplant. *Maximus est, plerumque in ligno*; the biggest man is usually a tree.

Similarly, when choosing from unknown players to compose your team, do not automatically choose the guy who drills all his warm-up jump shots; remember the ancient dictum, *Dum non est bonum et qui custos est vis pressionis cogente*; he who looks good when there is no pressure will wilt under pressure.

Unless there is some reason having to do with dislike and the urge to commit battery, do not seek to cover a guy who is clearly better than you. Choose a guy roughly your size and burl or lack thereof. If possible, watch him play the game before your game, and note if he only uses one hand, if he never drives, if he always stupidly veers away from picks, if he dislikes being crunched by picks, if he has favorite shooting spots, if he actually plays a lick of defense, and if he has the slightest acquaintance with the concept of an assist. In short, *Si omnino rutrum*, see if he is a total tool.

The first time a guy holds your arm or shirt or shorts on defense, you must sternly inform him that he must cease, without, if possible, using foul and reprehensible language. The second time and all times thereafter you may chop violently at his hand, seeking, if possible, to detach it from his forearm. *Qui me teret*; he who holds me will bruise.

If you have the ball on the break, and this last basket will win the game, and you have not one but two guys open for decent shots, and one of those guys is your brother, look directly at the guy who is not your brother, and then deliver the ball instead to your brother, as if presenting a savory morsel on a silver tea tray, so that your brother catches the pass and lays it in smoothly, winning the game, because *Omnibus est amor*, love is where it's at; which you already knew.

Llegamos Próximo!

Walking past a basketball court the other day I heard a guy say *We got next!*, which sent me into a reverie about the lingua franca of basketball, the common utterances, the ubiquitous phrases, the words that are said by players all over the world, albeit in different tongues and dialects, so that even if you are playing ball in Spain or Uruguay, and someone says *Llegamos próximo!*, you can tell from the firm bravura of the way the words are said, the clear and patent claiming-of-territory tone, that the guy is saying *We got next!*, which means My guys will play the winners of the game at hand, and anyone else who thinks *they* are going to play the next game will have to dicker with me about that.

There is *My bad*, which means sorry, gents, stupid pass, my mistake, mea culpa, and there is *Little help!*, which is what you call to people on the next court or the tennis courts or the baseball field or in the river rowing when your ball escapes the friendly confines of your court and sprints into their vicinity, and there is *Shoot that!*, said to someone who is inarguably open but reluctant by nature or religion to shoot even a wide-open eight-footer from the lane that God help us all a toddler could hit with his eyes closed, and there is *Pick left* or *Pick right*, which is what you call out to your teammate who is about to crash into a pick that he is not watching out for quite as assiduously as he should, and there is *Yo!* and *Ball!* and even occasionally, unbelievably, *I'm open!*, which is what dolts and fools shout when they want the ball, even though you have already seen the cold fact that they are *not* open, and will *never* be open if they stand around waving and calling for the ball, and you would not pass it to them even if they *were* open, because who wants to reward the kind of guy who stands there waving frantically for the ball and actually *calling to you for the ball?* Who would reward such behavior? Plus that kind of guy is usually wearing wristbands, which is just disturbing.

There is that most delicious of phrases spoken on a basketball court, *Who's got that guy?*, which means something much closer to The guy who just scored ten straight points is your guy and you are playing the most candy-ass lazy ludicrous defense of all time and we, your friendly teammates, hope and pray you will make even a modicum of effort on the defensive end sometime in this century, or we will replace you with that toddler who hit the eight-footer with his eyes closed. There is *Good game*, which sometimes means what it says but sometimes means something else altogether, and there are rude and vulgar things said that I don't need to go into here although it is interesting to me how common certain insults are no matter the speaker's culture or language or race or ethnicity or nationality or age or economic status or level of education or zip code or religious affiliation or lack thereof, and there is *Foul*, and *That was a foul*, and *That was a savage and untoward foul*, and *That was assault and battery with malicious intent*, and *Why don't you just use a stick next time*, and *If you foul me like that again I will hit you with a Buick Park Avenue*, and then there are all the things commonly said to referees, which we will skip over because who needs to wade in the mud, am I right?

Then there are things that are said after the game, in friendly or bitter tones—sometimes, interestingly, long after the game, sometimes even *years* after the game, such as recently when my friend Bill leaned over to me as we were having a very pleasant dinner with sockeye salmon and a terrific pinot gris, and said quietly *You stepped out of bounds*, which was a reference to a game that took place thirty years ago, in which I did *not* step out of bounds, and even if I *did* step out of bounds, which I did not, I was *pushed out*, which is, unquestionably, a foul, though I did not, as I have noted, step out of bounds, much.

Weatherball

I have played basketball in the snow; in Chicago I went up to the local playground one Sunday afternoon, to shoot around in the swirling snow, and a terrific gust of wind from the lake caught my first shot and blew it over the backboard and down Halsted Street so fast and so far that I thought I was going to have to catch a bus to retrieve it, but luckily a guy stopped it with his car door near Cornelia Avenue.

I have played in mist, and fog, and soft rain, and gentle rain, and hammering rain, and one time in a thunderstorm that we thought we could outlast until a bolt of lightning hit the light stanchion above us and we all ran like hell for one of the dugouts on the baseball field. One guy actually dove like a guy would dive into a foxhole in the movies but he got hung up on the little skirt of dirt on the edge of the dugout and he got a mouthful of clay and a few minutes later he found a waterlogged cricket in his hair.

I have played in a hailstorm, which I remember most for the utterly weird sensation of watching hailstones the size of marbles bounce off the shaved head of the grim guy defending me; that was not something I had seen before, or ever expect to see again. I remember wanting to laugh but this guy was not in a laughing mood so we just played on until the court got too slick. Still, though, occasionally I remember hailstones making a riveting plinking sound on his skull and then bouncing surprisingly high in every direction; it was like his brain was launching troops of cold white marbles, which *sounds* funny, but he didn't think it was.

I have played in a sleet-storm, with my brothers, at the basket on our garage, and I remember laughing so hard we couldn't stop, and one of my brothers, whom I shouldn't name here in public because of the audacity of the claim but it was Tommy, *claiming* he hit a lefty hook from over the little addition to the house where our grandmother lived, and over the clothesline, and over the lilac bushes, which is just faintly possible, given the fact that he was very good ballplayer, but was highly unlikely, as it's a totally blind shot, but on the other hand it was sleeting so thoroughly that we couldn't tell if a shot went in or not, so it might have.

I have played buffets and dervishes of whirling dust and sand. I have played in windstorms so terrific that birds seemed to be working furiously just to hold their parking spots in the air, and any shot from more than a foot away from the basket was sure to be blown around the court, such that a park employee standing fifty feet away innocently trying to sneak a cigarette would suddenly be beaned by a ball that had begun its journey as a short jump shot from the lane on Court One but now was a missile headed right for the guy on Court Two just as he finally got his cigarette lit inside the cupped cave of his hands. It was unbelievably windy that day but the guy's angry roar carried surprisingly well against the wind, much better than you would expect. I don't remember exactly what he said but I do remember that he said it firmly. I supposed that he was yelling at us because he thought we had deliberately beaned him, but one of the guys I was playing with speculated that he was yelling because he had swallowed a burning cigarette, which is not something you ever want to do, and an excellent reason why smoking cigarettes is a dangerous and unhealthy habit that should be avoided.

Dribblage

When I was a teenager I spent one entire summer, June through August, dribbling a basketball at least two hours a day, seven days a week, alternating left and right hands, while walking, running, jogging, sprinting, and even once backpedaling, just to see if it could be done, which it essentially cannot, and why would you need to dribble while backpedaling anyway? Yet I tried that, and I tried dribbling while riding a bicycle, which was pointless but hilarious, and I dribbled while being assaulted by two younger brothers to simulate defensive traps, and I dribbled while wearing ankle weights to simulate heavy-legged exhaustion, and I dribbled with sunglasses on to train myself not to look at the ball while dribbling, and I spent hours racing up and down courts dribbling behind my back and between my legs, and I practiced dribbling while skidding and sliding on the court, for a moment would come, I knew it, when I would need to keep my dribble alive even after being shoved or tripped, and I swore I would be ready for that moment.

I dribbled on the courts behind schools and temples. I dribbled down avenues and lanes and streets and trails and byways. I dribbled into and out of highway tunnels just to hear the cool booming sound. I dribbled along pathways and sidewalks and public thoroughfares. One afternoon I dribbled for a while along the Long Island Rail Road tracks until I heard a faint thunderous roar in the distance and I hopped off hurriedly and dribbled home. I dribbled my ball and my brother's ball and a ball I stole from the churchyard and even once a volleyball just to see if it could be done, which it essentially cannot. I once dribbled into a delicatessen and then out again hurriedly when the owner shouted and lurched out from behind the counter brandishing a kielbasa.

Did my maniacal dribbling drive my family insane? Heavens, yes. My mother many times ejected me for dribbling infractions, and my father many times glanced at me over the lip of his newspaper, which in his case was tantamount to roaring, and my sister shrieked and gibbered, and the local dogs blubbered and raged, and even the polite lady next door once asked if I could possibly desist my basketball *rehearsal*, as she called it, after sunset, as her husband was exhausted when he came home from long day of being an engineer on bridges in the city, and his repose was crucial to the family fortunes, so would I be a dear and keep that in mind?

I look back now at that peculiar boy, dribbling down one street after another, sprinting up and down one court after another, and while I see that he was a crazy person, a nut, a goof (and this is not even to mention the ankle weights and the sunglasses and the dribbling-while-sliding-on-asphalt thing), I also have to laud his lunacy. He wanted to be a better ballplayer so badly that he spent two hours a day (minimum—there were plenty of days when I got in more hours, and yes, I recorded my hours in a notebook) practicing this one crucial skill, so that he would be infinitesimally better at the game he loved above all others. He would never be great at the game, never be famous at it, never make a penny at it, but he loved it so that his hard work at it was the most airy and pleasant play. There was something good and true and even wise in that; something fine, something subtle, something that would be wonderfully eloquent, if we could only find the words.

The Suicide Sprint

Another ubiquitous aspect of every basketball practice was, and probably still is, the suicide sprint, in which the entire team lines up on the baseline, and, on command, usually a piercing whistle from the coach, who is secretly deeply glad that he is not running suicides, sprints to the foul line, bends to touch same, and back to the baseline, and to half court, and ditto, and the other foul line, and ditto, and then the whole court, and then rest, for a moment, unless you are gagging in the corner, or you are the slowest guys, who will finish the drill long after the greyhounds do.

What this drill was supposed to sharpen, exactly, is a mystery to me; I remember asking this of a coach once, and his answer was entertainingly all over the map, from heart rate to response to whistles to team camaraderie to muscle memory; I particularly remember him saying *muscle memory*, for I had the temerity even then, at age twelve, to note that nowhere in my experience of the game was I required to bend and touch a line on the court during a game or a scrimmage, and in fact it seemed to me that pausing to bend and touch a line on the court would be a *bad* thing during a game, because it would take me right out of the play, and how would that be a good thing, so why exactly are we doing this drill?

Yes, of course the coach made us do another set of sprints because I was mouthing off, as he said, and getting lippy, and horsing around, and being a clubhouse lawyer. I remember that last phrase, too, because none of us had ever heard it and three of us burst out laughing and yes, we all ran another set of sprints for that too.

Suicide sprints, though, were a game within a game, in a sense. In tryouts, in early practices, and indeed all through the year, winning the sprints was a surefire way to catch the coach's eye, just as finishing last was a sure way to reap his ire. Most guys learned to finish in the middle of the pack, pacing themselves to save energy for the actual game or practice, and indeed in many cases conspiring beforehand to finish together as an anonymous gaggle staggering over the line. Some guys were brilliant cheaters, hinting or feinting at bending to touch the line, or elbowing another guy to throw him off-stride, or cutting a guy off in the home stretch and angling slightly toward the coach so as to make your victory obvious. Other guys, usually the bigger guys, would jog through the whole drill, knowing they were doomed to finish at the back of the pack anyway, and seeing no reason to expend energy to move up one or two niggling slots. Other guys evaded the drill altogether with a wide panoply of excuses, from dizziness to water breaks to sneaker malfunction to a rolled ankle; I remember one guy in particular who had the most amazing ability to be limping when the whistle blew for sprints and then springy as could be once practice started. But then it was a Catholic school gymnasium, and any number of miracles were possible, such as for example the time when the coach made the malingerer run suicides anyway, and he had to step into the janitor's closet afterward and gag for a while. I remember that particularly because the rest of us were happy that he was gagging and also something about the acoustics of the janitor's closet made it seem like his gagging was ten times louder than gagging usually gets to be.

I still cannot quite see the point of suicide sprints, when there are so many other drills that foment and sharpen quickness and agility and swift reaction and good instinct and proper form and positioning; and while I cannot think of them with affection, because of the whole gagging thing, I can remember them with a smile, and see the worst player on the team consistently winning the sprints and feeling damned good about it, too; and the big guys lumbering in last and not feeling the slightest guilt about it, nor did they care a whit about the lash of the coach's ire; and the guy who played the least minutes of us all winning a sprint one day by committing an egregious foul on our cocky star, just as our coach turned his head to bark at the lumbering big guys, so that the coach did not see the shove, and he congratulated the grinning winner, and talked him up to us as a model suicide sprinter, as our star whined and whimpered, and there was a ripple of quiet laughter all around the gym, a wonderful and unforgettable sound.

Cut

The first time you ever get cut from a team is when you are sixteen. You spot a piece of paper on the wire-shot glass of the gymnasium door. You crowd around the door with the other kids. You glance real quick, hoping your name will leap or shout, but it doesn't and you have a little wriggle of awful in your belly and you press closer on the excuse that you have thick spectacles and you run your finger down the twelve names and you see names you expected and names you didn't and Not You. The names are all typed on the coach's old typewriter which screws up the letter y so it looks more like w so you check again from the top looking for *Dowle, Brian* and then you check again reading up from the bottom this time just in case some weird thing happened because you wear thick spectacles and the gym door has this thick old shimmery glass and maybe the two densities of glass cancel each other out or something. By now other kids are shoving you because you have inarguably been camped by the door for too long and you allow yourself to get shoved to the edge of the pack and you assume an airy casual I don't care face and you get ready to say *Man I didn't really want to be on the team anyway it would cut into my social life heh heh heh* if anyone asks but the other kids are either finding their names or turning away rattled and trying to get their masks on hurriedly like you are.

It's hard to get your mask on while you are walking so you duck into the men's room but there's another kid in there who is having a terrible time with his mask and you don't want to cry either so you duck back out and keep moving.

His name is Fred and he is the kid you once had to share a jersey with when you both were the twelfth guy on a twelve-man team when you were twelve years old and his family was poor or sick or something and after he wore the jersey he never washed it and he smelled like dog barf so when you got the jersey for your game your mom washed it before *and* after so during the season the jersey got noticeably lighter in color than the other jerseys and you were always afraid someone would notice but no one did.

By now you absolutely *know* you are going to cry and this is a disaster because it means you are a baby and not a man and you are seeking refuge which turns out to be shockingly the backstage door of the school theater. You duck in this door and hear the mumble of some awful crap like Molière on stage but amazingly there to your right is the low door that leads actually under the stage which looks right now like the most alluring place in the world.

You close the low door behind you carefully and kneel down and cry like hell and then you run through all the possible reasons for being cut like the coach hates Catholic guys or hates guys with glasses or hates guys with Irish names or he was too drunk to see at tryouts or he was paid off by a dad to choose another guy or there are twelve better players. You run through each of the twelve guys and consider trying to be honest if they are better and no way they are *all* better but you can actually see how someone uninformed and careless might *think* they are all better even the guy missing a part of his pinky he lost in a boating accident how a guy without all his fingers could make the team and not you is a mystery but there it is.

By now you have stopped crying but even as you shudder to a stop you are quietly amazed that crying is an autopilot thing and you cannot stop crying by telling yourself to stop crying; you only stop when the crying is finished with itself. You remember learning this when you were twelve and your grandmother died but that was long ago when you were twelve.

Suddenly the low door opens and you crouch down into a corner of the understage where there are some things that look like couches where virgins get deflowered in Molière plays and for an instant before the door closes again you see to your amazement it is Fred, who must have had the same idea to duck into a place where he could cry like hell. You notice he still smells like dog barf. You notice this more and more as the minutes slog past and he finishes his crying. You think about maybe saying something to the poor guy, I mean he just got cut, too, although he damn well should have been cut, he couldn't score if you locked him in the gym alone for a week, but you don't, because that would be weird, and also because as you realize later you were frightened by kindness then, thinking it weakness, and how wrong you were, and still occasionally are.

After a while Fred left and you waited a sufficient number of minutes to let him escape, and then you escaped also, noting dully as you crept away that the same French drivel was still being committed above you, and when you got back out in the hallway it was empty and the afternoon was getting to be dusk. You walked back toward the gym for a moment until you heard a thunder of basketballs as the team trickled out onto the floor for its first practice and then you turned and walked the other way toward the south door of the school. For a moment you thought you were screwed and you would have to walk the mile home, all buses having left long ago, but then amazingly Fred came by in his car and said hey you need a lift and you said sure thanks man and all the way home you both lied about why you were still at school. Years later you realized this was another jersey you shared with Fred, the way both of you lied like hell all the way home. Maybe sometimes lies are kindness. Even his car smelled like dog barf but when a guy gives you a ride when you really need a ride you don't say anything about that.

Conscious Fouls

A Note

In basketball there are uncountable ways to foul a guy unconsciously, from awkwardness or misposition or laziness or recklessness or foolishness or weariness; in fact you can foul a guy unconsciously without actually fouling him, if the referee is out of position, or grumpy, or distracted, or making the classic phantom call that referees do sometimes, when they blow the whistle because you should, by all rights, *have* committed a foul on that play, but you miraculously didn't, yet he will assume you did, even though you didn't, and you will surely earn a technical foul when you point out, in a calm and reasonable manner, that he is a horse's ass of epic proportions and that is why women don't like him and guys hit him in the back of the head with an errant pass once a season on principle.

But one thing ballplayers never talk about is all the *conscious* ways to commit fouls, of which there are many, of all different shapes and sizes and flavors. There are the light experimental fouls, which you commit judiciously, trying to discover the day's transgression line, which is different for every referee; some referees will whistle almost any contact, while others will allow battery with pumpkins and mammals and snow boots. There are message fouls, which are sly and subtle ways to inform an opponent that no, he cannot set up permanent camp in the lane, and no, he cannot crack your hands and wrists and arms, and no, he cannot grab your shirt, and yes, you are going to damn well get around that corner by using your elbow as a sharp lever if necessary, and yes, you are going to continue to drive the lane even if he flops and fakes so dramatically that the stock market goes down, and yes, you are going to slip his pick all night long even if there is to be a brief intense grapple at the passage point every time.

Then there are the light fouls designed not to be seen by the referee, such as the way you gently touch the shooting elbow of a shooter just as he is releasing his shot, secure in the knowledge that the referee is looking at the ball, not at your hand; and the way you gently rest your hand on the midsection of a shooter taking a fall-away shot, and give him a helpful shove in the direction that he is falling away, so that what began as a ten-foot fall-away becomes a thirteen-foot fall-away; and the way that you make a seemingly valiant effort to arrive on the scene of a hook shot, and having failed to arrive swiftly enough to actually get a hand up to contest the shot, politely tuck your shoulder and deliver a thunderous blow to the shooter's chest, which often does affect the hook shot, not to its benefit.

Then there are the conscious fouls that you commit with vengeful intent; I suppose these are also message fouls, but they are not the conversational fouls as above, by which players communicate certain opinions and policy stances; these are more like messages delivered in large bold type, so that not only the recipient of the foul is informed of the message, but pretty much everyone else in the gym. Among this sort of foul is the high elbow, which is a blunt message to cease and desist whatever it is that the recipient has been doing, usually flailing his own elbows or setting overly savage picks; and there is the ostensible attempt at a steal that may or may not get part of the ball, but assuredly gets every millimeter of the recipient's hands, with a resounding crack, which is usually a message about how *someone* should stop swiping at the ball without the slightest hope of stealing it.

There are, of course, other more egregious and dangerous fouls in basketball, but those sorts of fouls are vulgar and mean and have no place in the game, which are rightly instantly punished, often with ejection or a fist in the face. I feel that the less we talk about those fouls the better, for they are, like narcissistic demagogues, things that thrive on attention; so let us ignore them, and perhaps they will wither away, which will be a welcome benefit to the greatest of games, and to this wild and lovely world.

Mr. Wilson's Hat

Our coach, Mr. Wilson, had been a major in the United States Army, and had a chip on his shoulder about long hair and beards, even the awful earnest scraggly embarrassing first beards of his teenage players, so it was particularly galling to him to have a starting five that featured four ponytails and a beard, although that beard, covering most of the face of our center, was such a dense thicket that you couldn't see his mouth, which was entertaining to his teammates because he kept up a lewd chatter all game long, and the referees were constantly looking suspiciously at Mr. Wilson, who wouldn't know lewd chatter if it shook him by the hand and asked him to tea, even though he had been an officer in the United States Army, and served in the Korean War.

Our ponytails flapping as we sprinted up and down the court drove him nuts, and our wild chaotic style of play drove him nuts, and our calling timeout once a game to adjust our headbands drove him nuts, and once a game one of us would deliberately drive him nuts by committing an incredibly ridiculous turnover just to hear him make that strangled hopeless sound in his throat, and we would hide his dapper fedora hat to drive him nuts, and he kept after us anyway, practice after practice, game after game, even with all these things driving him nuts, because he was actually a good guy and a good coach, although we didn't see that then, and we called him simply The Man, and fought his ungentle instructions to make the most of our talents, and shape our creative energies, and try to play *well*, rather than simply play *fast*, which we preferred to do, for reasons that were clear then but now seem selfish.

But it is a single moment from that season that comes back to me now, and oddly it flooded back on me this evening, as I watched a boy lace up his sneakers for a basketball game. I was superstitious when I played for Mr. Wilson, and I ran through pre-game drills in certain set ways, and changed socks and headbands according to how well I had played the game before, and many more tiny silly things like that, even in practice; and one evening, before practice, as I laced and relaced my sneakers to get them exactly right, while humming my lacing-and-relacing song, Mr. Wilson sat down next to me and started talking.

This was highly unusual for him, as generally he kept a dignified or annoyed distance from us, and it was doubly unnerving for me because he was messing with my lacing and relacing ritual, but for once I had the wit to stop battling and just listen to him.

I used to do that too, when I was in the Army, he said. I used to lace and relace my boots before any kind of event. I got into the habit in boot camp, I think. Probably a way to calm down. One time I remember I was asleep when guys attacked across a river on a bridge they'd built just *below* the surface of the water, how smart was that? So we had to hurry. But I laced and relaced my boots. I *had* to. My guys were screaming at me to hurry up. We laughed about it afterwards. So there you go. Took me *years* to stop lacing and relacing. What a *relief* to get into civilian shoes again. Now I know why God invented loafers, so we don't have to lace and relace, you know what I mean? Well, no, you don't, but perhaps someday you will. Alright, let's get going. We only have the gym until eight tonight, there's a musical rehearsal or something, we don't want to be here for *that*, do we? And that's Sister Agnes, a stickler for time.

I remember sitting there startled for a moment, after he jumped up to go bark at the other players, and I'd like to report that I jumped up and ran after him and said something, anything—something as piercing as listen, Mr. Wilson, thank you for going to war, nobody ever says thanks for that, or as innocuous as hey, Mr. Wilson, that's cool that you are a lacing-and-relacing nut also. But I didn't. I sat there for moment thinking about how creatively devious an underwater bridge would be if you wanted to get across a river at night and murder some unsuspecting guys, and then I got back into my lacing and relacing ritual, and then practice started, and while we were supposed to spend that whole practice focusing on getting the ball inside to the big guys at the *start* of a possession, so they could dish it back out if they were bottled up and we could spread the floor, pretty soon we lost interest in the theme and started hoisting up silly shots, and trying to run fast breaks off even made shots, and making egregious turnovers just to see if we could get Mr. Wilson to make that strangled hopeless sound in his throat, which eventually he did. So we thought it was a pretty good practice, all things considered, made all the better by a guy hiding Mr. Wilson's dapper fedora hat in the men's room. As I remember Mr. Wilson finally found his hat just after Sister Agnes had given him a bitter look because it was after eight o'clock and he was late getting his team out of the gym.

A Note on Shots

I have played basketball with soccer balls, volleyballs, kickball balls, tether-balls, and even once a tennis ball, although that game did not last long, as the ball was incredibly difficult to dribble properly unless you were nearly horizontal to the ground, which is not a position from which you arise and vault easily into the stratosphere for a jump shot.

I have not technically played a basketball game with a golf ball, though I have taken shots with one, and with a baseball, and a cricket ball, and a rugby ball, and a football, and a wiffle ball, and a beach ball, and clods of dirt, and rocks and stones, and a stale bagel, and a baseball cap, and a golf club (just to see if you can cartwheel it through the hoop, which it turns out you can, if you spend an inordinate amount of time trying to do so). I have taken shots with Frisbees and plastic cups and dog bowls and bright plastic beach buckets. I once hit a long set shot with a small wooden bowl and won one dollar for the feat. I once hit a short hook shot with a paperback copy of Saul Bellow's *The Adventures of Augie March*, which is surely a sentence never written before in this lovely and tumultuous world. I once contemplated taking a middling set shot with the carcass of a squirrel but was persuaded this was a poor idea, which it was.

I have many times tossed balls of wadded paper through toy hoops and into bins and buckets across the room, sometimes deftly or accidentally banking the shot off a desk or a wall, and one time off an editorial colleague. I once flipped a plastic coffee cup over my shoulder through a toy hoop from eight feet away while talking to a college literature professor, whose caterpillar eyebrows leapt up remarkably as he saw the feat accomplished—that man had eyebrows like tracts of the most dense and verdant Amazonian jungle. Twice that I remember I walked into someone's office, and noticed that he had a tiny toy basketball hoop perched on the door, and instantly, without thinking, in a classic mammalian case of sight leading immediately to instinctive act, reached into my pocket and tossed my car keys through the hoop, and capered and gamboled around, crowing and boasting as if it were the buzzer-beater that just won the league title.

But the one shot that I remember best, of all the many thousands of shots I have taken at basketball baskets, with hundreds of balls of every sort and shape, leather and rubber and various horrifying indeterminate plastics, is a shot taken one day on the playground of the grade school where my three children were educated. It was a mossy moist gray dripping Oregon afternoon, and my twin sons, perhaps age ten, were playing basketball with their fellow ruffians as I walked long musing meditative laps around the adjacent soccer field. By happy chance, as I rounded the edge of the field nearest to the basketball court, the ball bounced away from the players and toward me; without pausing in my shamble I picked it up on the bounce, set my feet, and launched a ridiculous forty-footer, from a terrible angle, through the gathering mist—a hopeless shot, a ludicrous shot, a shot showing breathtaking arrogance that it was even attempted, when I should have sensibly tossed the ball back to the players—and of course it dropped cleanly through the basket, and I shuffled on, grinning, and behind me I heard the most wonderful joyous thrilling satisfying sound a father can hear, other than the gentle splash of his children arriving wetly in this world: my sons whooping and crowing and laughing, delighted by and proud of their dad.

Scribbling and Dribbling

A Note

In recent years I have become absorbed by the startling basketball ped-
igrees of many of the Northwest's finest writers—Sherman Alexie and
Robin Cody and Barry Lopez were all high-school stars, David Duncan
was a spring-loaded rat-ball forward, and even Ken Kesey, for all his fame
as a wrestler, is reputed to have been a decent, if foul-prone, hoop player.
Taking this line of thought out for a stroll, I started wondering where
other fine writers would fit on basketball teams—Oregon's sturdy and
sinewy John Daniel, for example, once a logger, is clearly a rooted center, and the tiny and brilliant Ursula Le Guin, deft and inventive and confident, is clearly a point guard. Molly Gloss, willowy and efficient, looks
like a smooth forward to me; the effervescent Marc Acito looks like the
fizzy wild-eyed guard you want leaping off the bench and energizing a
dull game; Tim Egan, with his all-round skill set, can play three positions;
the late Ivan Doig and Tom Robbins, let's say, are guards who check into
the game together, the disciplined Doig calming the wildly talented but
infinitely combustible Robbins . . .

The more I did this with Northwest writers for sheer entertainment
(Stewart Holbrook distracting the refs and the other team with a string
of witty remarks, Beverly Cleary letting dogs romp on the court, Chuck
Palahniuk getting into fistfights, Bernard Malamud playing the first quarter and then fleeing to Vermont), the more it seemed to be oddly revela-
tory of characteristics of their work, and the more I itched to apply the fil-
ter to American literature at large. I mean, doesn't it say something about
Barry Lopez's eerie control of his prose, its cadenced dignity, that he once

controlled the ball and the rhythm of the game? Doesn't it reveal something of Duncan's soaring imaginative leaps as a writer when you realize he was a wild lanky floating egret of a ballplayer?

So I see Saul Bellow, un-tall and burly and cocky, as a point guard, a sort of Jewish Chris Paul; and Ernest Hemingway, all muscles and glower and attitude, as a power forward, a kind of literary Maurice Lucas; and Mark Twain, who did everything well, as a literary Oscar Robertson, dominating smoothly without seeming to expend much energy (ah, the art of artlessness). And off we go, dreaming: John Updike as Kobe Bryant, unbelievably great sometimes but somehow just a tad too solipsistic; and Flannery O'Connor dropping one killer dart after another from the corners, a female Ray Allen; and John Steinbeck toiling quietly and consistently for years, always excellent and hardly ever dramatic, the Tim Duncan of American letters; and Dave Eggers as Kevin Durant, talented and generous, and Annie Dillard as LeBron James, great right from the start and maybe one of the best ever . . .

We could, of course, play this game endlessly, with writers who were better players than writers, like the late James Carroll, or writers who were good players who later wrote beautifully about the game itself (John McPhee and John Edgar Wideman are probably all alone there), but this line of thinking always ends up, at least for me, with a dream of the day when there will come a young writer who will make one startling book after another about basketball. It's the most sinuous, quicksilver, flowing, graceful game there is, the most American in its generosity of scoring and its gentle violence, and there will arise a writer to match it, I hope . . .

Hints and Intimations

A Note

My friend Tommy Crotty was a terrific basketball player who started his career in dusty cramped wooden Catholic school gymnasiums in New York, gyms that at their best had not been swept or mopped for weeks and sometimes months, gyms that often featured windows with padlocks and wire screens nailed over them, gyms with windows so ancient and dirty that feeble bars of sunlight could only trickle in, gyms where spectators had to sit on the rickety wooden stage to watch him play, gyms that were sometimes not gyms at all but school auditoriums with smooth stony linoleum floors across which you slid as if playing on ice, gyms with no locker rooms or showers, gyms with scorekeepers who were twelve years old and referees who were too old to run up and down and who simply stationed themselves at midcourt to watch the action; but he ended his career as the starting point guard for a college team, which is a remarkable thing to say, for Tommy was not tall, nor was he muscular, nor was he laser-fast, nor was he liquid-quick, nor was he a feared shooter capable of drilling shots from anywhere at any time, although he did have an evil little boyish teardrop shot he would hoist suddenly when he got into the lane, which never missed, and which drove opposing big guys insane; many times, in the second halves of games in which Tommy had hit two or three of these little fling shots, I would hear inarguably foul language from the other team's center and forwards, who thought that they should be able to block that shot easily, but never could quite get to it in time; even now I think Tommy would take this shot sometimes just to needle them; he never had much respect for big guys, whom he collectively called Meat, on the court, and toyed with them sometimes for entertainment, as a mouse toys with a cat.

But he was devious, and subtle, and deft, and no player I have ever seen was more entertainingly great at suggesting one thing with his body and then doing another. He was a master at hints and intimations, at beginning a move and then switching gears altogether. In technical terms he was a wizard with show fakes, pump fakes, ball fakes, look-away passes, backdoor cuts, all the various and sundry theatrical aspects of the game; but it is his deeper artistry that I want to explore for a moment, for more and more I think he was a psychological and sociological brilliance, an artist who used opposing players' expectations and assumptions against them, and always cheerfully; I conclude now, thinking back on years of playing with Tommy, that his greatest pleasure on the court was a successful fake, more so than baskets or assists or victories.

A twitch of his head one way, as his body slid the other; a shoulder fake in one direction, and a sudden spin in the other; the hint of a shot, and then a long pause as his defender sailed past, flailing desperately, and then an easy set shot; or the best of all, his sleight of hand with his hands. He knew that defenders were alert to movement, and it was and is the rare defender who focuses his attention on the chest, as coaches endlessly teach, on the theory that where the chest goes the player will go also. No; defenders, and particularly defenders assigned to Tommy, were high-strung and keyed to a fantastic pitch, and he knew this, and played with their attentiveness as a cat would play with a mouse. He would shoot out his right hand, then dribble left, and his defender would leap out of his way, following the right hand like a falcon after meat. He would present the ball suddenly to the startled defender, who would reach for it with both hands like a toddler accepting a pumpkin, only to hear the ball suddenly whistle past his ear, on its way to an open man under the basket. He would pretend to throw a pass to his left, but retain the ball at the last second, and again the defender would leap after the pass that had not been thrown. I once saw him make a move that he later acknowledged he had borrowed from the great Pete Maravich; tossing the ball in the air, whipping one hand under it, and then snatching and passing it in the other direction with his other hand, this time as his defender just stood there gaping. That play I remember particularly well, for I was the boy the pass flew toward, and I was just as fuddled as the defender, and I did not catch it cleanly, and it skittered out of bounds, and Tommy grinned at me as we ran back on defense, for which I am still grateful.

They expect certain things, he said to me once, and I try to give them what they expect, for an instant, because they are so *sure* it will happen, and so *ready* for it to happen, and have thought so much about what they will do *when* it happens, that when I make it happen, for an instant, they are sort of delighted. It's like they are waiting for me to tell them a story they love and when I begin the story they are so ready to finish it that they cannot wait for me. I am not trying to embarrass anyone, as people have said here and there. I am not trying to make anyone look bad. In a sense I am helping them pay closer attention, you know? I mean, I am not going to overpower anyone, and it's their own fault when I offer them a fake and they bite. Now I have gotten to the point where I am careful about what fake comes when, you know? Like I will save a really productive one for a moment when I really need it. Or sometimes I let a guy block my shot, or seem to, just to set him up for a fake later on the same play. It has to be a chess game for me because I am not going to blow by anybody. I have to either find space or make space, and I am not quick enough to force it, so I have to move my defender around somehow. I love picks and screens because they give me even more tools to play with. I actually love moving without the ball, because defenders, no matter how good they are, just do not pay as close attention to a guy without the ball as they do to the guy with the ball, so you can move your defender around as you like. Backdoor cuts are another thing I save to use once in a game, or maybe twice if I have a real inattentive guy. Interestingly the best athletes are often the most inattentive guys. Other guys, like you for example, are just not very interested in defense. Defense to them is like homework they have to do before the pleasure of offense. So a guy like that, you make him work, you make him wait, you extend his homework, and his attention will flag, and there's my space. The most fun games of all for me are ones where I get a good defender, and he crowds me, he's in my shirt, he's real clear that he's shutting me down, his mission is closing me down. I love that, man. That kind of guy is so intent on playing good defense that

I can bring all the fakes out and have some fun. That's the guy you invent new stuff for. You turn your mind off and let it roll and stuff happens. A guy like that, I don't want the game to end. You almost pray for overtime, and for both of you to have four fouls, and there's a minute left, and he's right in your grill, and I get the ball on the break, and . . . man, I love ball. You know what I mean. Well, *you* don't know what I mean about defense, but you know what I mean about ball. No game is ever the same. No play is ever the same. You surprise even yourself. It's like the game has surprises in it and players haven't found them all. Maybe there's no end to the things that can happen in a game. That could be. Wouldn't that be cool? That would most definitely be cool. Let's get some guys and run this afternoon at the park. I know—let's you and me play only left-handed and see what happens. Want to?

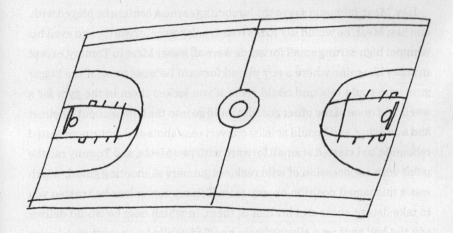

Meat

My friend Tommy Crotty, who was a terrific basketball player in New York and went on to play college ball and be a cheerful husband and excellent dad before the idiot who just died in Abbottabad murdered him and thousands of other children of all ages on September Eleventh, used to call every big guy he ever played with Meat.

Hey, Meat, he would say to the lumbering earnest centers he played with, and hey, Meat, he would say to his tree-trunk power forwards, and even his whippet high-strung small forwards were all lesser Meat to Tommy, except in cases like mine where a guy played forward because none of the bigger guys who could rebound could score if you locked them in the gym for a week, and none of the other guards would go into the lane without a helmet and a crowbar, and I could at least convert easy shots and grab uncontested rebounds, so I started at small forward with two Meats, and Tommy ran the point with a succession of wild reckless gunners at shooting guard, which was a misnamed position on any team Tommy ran unless he trusted you to take decent shots and hit half of them, in which case he would deliver you the ball as if on a silver platter handled gently by an unctuous butler on Sunday.

He was a most amazing point guard, was Tommy Crotty, his name often all one word in the mouths of the coaches and refs and parents and fans who came to watch him slide like a grinning knife through what seemed like every team in the greater New York metropolitan area, *tommy-crotty*, you would even hear this odd word in churches and bars and one time at the police station, where there was a misunderstanding about an automobile until the sergeant realized that we played with *tommycrotty*, as he said, the word reverential in his mouth like he was talking about one of the lesser apostles. It turned out one of his kids was a ballplayer and the kid's team had gone up against our team and, hey, total respect for you other guys, I mean no decredation, said the sergeant, but our guys totally had your number except for your kid at the point, that kid is a magician, I never seen a kid do things like that with a basketball, and he is not the most athletic kid I seen either, which was true, Tommy was never going to be six feet tall and he was what his mother called husky, which is another word for unsculpted.

One time I asked Tommy why he called all the big guys Meat and he said it was just easier that way, that learning their names was pointless because they all responded to the same simple stimuli, and names were excessive in regard to big guys, who were not the brightest stars in the sky. They want the ball early, you know, said Tommy, I think to reassure themselves that they exist, so I get each Meat a basket early, and then they're *happy*, man. They are not the brightest bulbs in the galaxy. Once they score they are good for long stretches. Meat has short memories. Later in the half I get them another couple buckets each just to be sure they're awake. Otherwise I want them working for me, you know? Not worrying about scoring. I'll take care of the score, but I need Meat work done out there, and *you're* not going to do it, prancing around like a hairy ballerina. At least *you* don't yell for the ball, which is why I give it to you when you're open. Some guys actually *yell at me* for the ball, can you imagine? Now, Meat would *never* yell for the ball, they are better behaved than that, but once in a while a Meat will set up his tent in the hole and wave for the ball. I wave back, man. Can you imagine signaling *me* to give *you* the ball? You don't think *I* know where the ball should go? Jesus. I had a Meat once who was waving for the ball and I waved back and his face lit up and he shouted *Hey, Tommy!* This is why I call them Meat, man. We have had some good Meat here, remember that Meat with the ponytail, that guy worked his butt off and never said a word, and he got rewarded for it, didn't he? He got the ball regular. Sometimes I was so proud of him for working so hard I'd give him the ball every other time down. You never saw happier Meat. And to his credit he never got all artsy and cocky, neither. I think because the ball was probably a shiny new toy to him every time he saw it, you know. I mean, the guy was a *center*, you know, so you keep your standards reasonable, you know what I'm saying?

This was how Tommy talked to us in the gym and the playground but when he was talking to the coaches and refs and parents and fans who called him *tommycrotty* he used his Altar-Girl Voice, all polite and reasonable and thanking the Madonna for what small gifts he had been given and stuff like that. You could melt butter in the mouth that otherwise pretty much had only the words *Meat* and *Good game* in it. He didn't talk on the floor at all except after a game, when he was one of the few guys I ever knew who made a point of shaking every guy's hand on both teams and saying *Good game* and actually meaning it, which is rare, most guys don't mean it at all and they would totally give you the finger if people weren't watching.

Well, the reason I wanted to tell you about Tommy was more than the entertaining way he called all big guys Meat; it's about the time I absolutely hammered a guy on a blind pick in a game, and Tommy said something afterward that I've thought about a lot since he was murdered by the idiot in Abbottabad. The guy I clocked in that game was hammering Tommy the whole game, because basically Tommy was killing his team and the rest of us weren't, and this guy, I think his name was Rocco, figured he would cut the head off the snake, you know? So he bashed Tommy every chance he got, setting mean picks, cracking Tommy's hands and arms while supposedly going for the ball, really dropping the hammer on Tommy twice on drives to the basket, one time accidentally-on-purpose whipping a pass right in Tommy's face like the ball had slipped but it hadn't, and finally we'd had enough, and me and the Meat set up a blind back pick, which is an evil basketball way to exact vengeance on a guy, as he comes flying around the Meat pick, a pick he expects and has seen all game, and then runs smack into a second vicious pick that he did not expect, the second pick being me with an elbow aimed at his eye. Well, the guy went down in a heap, and there was a ruckus with coaches and dads yelling and stuff, but the ref had seen the way the guy was bashing Tommy, and he figured an eye for an eye, so that was that.

But that *wasn't* that, it turned out, because after the game Tommy read me the riot act, and told me never to do that again, not on his floor, or I would never see the ball again except in the shiny windows of sports stores, and more things like that. He said he understood why we had done it and he appreciated the thought but there was a right way and a wrong way to play and he would be damned if anyone on his team played the wrong way. I asked what about Rocco hammering him and he said screw him, a guy like that you just play harder and show him the error of his ways. I said that was stupid and guys like that were idiots and would never see the error of their ways and the best way to deliver a lesson to a guy like that was with your elbow in his eyeball, maybe two elbows. Tommy said you are not listening to me, which is disappointing, you are not Meat, try to pay attention, and remember I have the ball and you do not. There is a right way and a wrong way to play. We play the right way. Guys who play the wrong way will lose in the end. Are you listening to me? Do I have to write this down? The way to teach a guy who plays the wrong way is to play the right way. *They want you to play the wrong way.* Get it? They are not the brightest bulbs in the galaxy. So the way to really drive them bonkers and make them go home and punch the wall is to play the right way. Firstly it is the only way to play and secondly it gives them a chance to wake up although me personally I would not bet the house on that. Are you listening to me?

Yes, I was. Yes.

Hoooop

And speaking of basketball, a wild flood of memories washes me along grinning this morning.

First: the moment on a playground in Brooklyn when I drove the baseline hard and soared to the basket to lay the ball in above the rim with a cool little flip of the fingers, and instead I got hammered thoroughly by two bigger stronger guys, a play I remember vividly as the moment I realized that (a) I was not actually big enough to be a forward, and (b) there were guys who were a *lot* better than me in the world, and (c) I was not good enough to play college ball, as I had thought I might. If guys in a pickup game with glass shards on the court could casually reject my best efforts, maybe journalism or crime was a better option—or both together, if I could get a job with Rupert Murdoch.

Second: a moment on a playground in New Mexico when my friend Pete and I stopped to play pickup with a bunch of Navajo boys who (a) were quicker than cougars and relentlessly energetic even after an hour of intense play whereas I wanted to go lie down in a cold creek for the rest of the afternoon, and (b) were awed by Pete, who was a solid 6'4" and 250 pounds but unbelievably deft for a guy who weighed an eighth of a ton. The thought of those boys swirling around Pete like a river around a rock stays with me even now.

Third: a moment on a playground deep in rural Ireland where the netless basket was too high and the court was made of pitted grass and awful mud and the ball was ancient beyond belief but my brothers and I battled all afternoon against local guys who were not great ballplayers but good heavens what athletes not at *all* afraid of physical play, it turned out. Afterwards one of them told me they were all members of the local hurling team.

Fourth: a moment in Australia when I stopped at a playground in Sydney and watched a pickup game among boys and girls who were maybe fifteen years old and one girl was so liquid-quick and shifty that the boys were annoyed at how much better she was but she did not care about their annoyance and she kept toying with them, which made me unaccountably happy. By then I was too old and creaky to shuck my coat and ask to step in for a while but I stood there under a gum tree thrilled that I could still read and feel and sense and decode and be delighted by the game even if I was not inside its glorious generous joyous swift flow any more.

Many fine things were invented in America, among them jazz and Mormonism and the blues and Flannery O'Connor and the zipper and Abraham Lincoln, but I do not forget that basketball was also invented here, one winter in Massachusetts, 124 years ago, or that the game now elevates and enlivens the world, and for that, this morning, we ought to be very proud, seems to me.

Out

You would think, if you were playing basketball on a court with out-of-bounds lines clearly and inarguably marked on the asphalt or concrete or maple surface, that when the guy you are defending steps on the line, or over the line, or so far over the line that it's like his foot took a vacation to the Canary Islands, that he would be clearly and inarguably out of bounds, which would count as an infraction of the rules, and cause possession to transfer to the other team, generally at the point of infraction; but this is not always so, not at all, and that is what I would like to ponder this morning, for the fact is that there are endless permutations of *out*, and many times when a guy is out but not out, which is a remarkable thing to write, but it is so, and is one of the reasons to love park or street basketball, where there are no referees except the players themselves, and no code except that which is generally agreed upon by the players, which is why such things as a guy being out but not out are possible, if not prevalent.

In park or street ball you call your own fouls, and what is or is not a foul is generally agreed upon, such that a direct bodily assault with malice aforethought is a foul, while deftly shoving and holding a guy while you are jockeying for rebounding position is not a foul. But the matter of guys stepping out of bounds is not at all as clear-cut, and depends more on the particular guys who are playing, and their characters and egos, and their predilections to fiction, and how annoyed they are at the score or at how they are being hammered by the guys they are supposed to be covering, and the status of their love lives or lack thereof, and sometimes, for all I can figure, the weather, or their plummeting stock portfolios; for I have seen defenders call a guy out of bounds when he clearly was not at all out of bounds and everyone else knew this, and I have seen out-of-bounds calls when one millimeter of a sneaker touched the line, and I have seen out-of-bounds calls when the only reason the guy with the ball went out of bounds is that his defender shoved him out of bounds with all his might.

On the other hand, when I played ball many years ago, I drove the baseline and stepped on the line, and over the line, and inarguably over the line, and egregiously over the line, and was not called out, for all sorts of reasons, one of which was my own adamant insistence that I had the eyes of a hawk and the balance of a falcon and always knew my exact position in the world and had *never* stepped out of bounds; a ludicrous claim that my friends occasionally found irritating, and rightly so, but which they also found more entertaining than frustrating, for the most part, for I got away with a thousand infractions, always without, I say with rue, the slightest hint of guilt on my part, although now that I think about it I remember my friends almost always grinning on the court—probably more at my goggle-eyed mania than I realized.

If you knew your opponent well, you would let him step on the line, or even over it, from affection and respect; or because you had actually given him a healthy surreptitious shove; or because it was a lovely day and he had made a spectacular move and it would be a small soul who would overrule that grace and creativity; or because you had committed the same infraction thrice in the last three minutes; or sometimes because the whole concept of boundary lines seemed fascist; or sometimes because the line itself was only a memory on the court, long faded from the scene, and marked now only in legend and estimation, and surely never to be repainted, not while this mayor was using park funds for vacations to the Canary Islands; and so it was that often out was not out at all, which is a lovely idea to end on, as mysterious and alluring as the game of basketball itself.

Common Scents

The *ball* smelled good—and I don't mean just the new balls fresh from heaven, from whence all basketballs come, but used balls also, even balls so old and worn that they shone; even those balls smelled like effort and friends and sweat and the dusty closets where they had to wait all day before being freed at last to soar.

And the shining gleaming wooden gymnasium floors smelled good, even when they were dense with dust, even when they had been too thickly waxed, and the occasional linoleum floor smelled good, even when it was littered with church circulars and pocked by high heels, and the outdoor courts smelled good, even when they were occasionally littered with pebbles and shards of glass and sparrow feathers and the desiccated feet of pigeons gobbled by falcons, and a guy I knew who had played a game on an aircraft carrier said even *that* court smelled good, probably because of the gentle sea breeze, not to mention the fact that he was playing ball instead of washing dishes, which is most of what he did in the Navy.

And new sneakers smelled good, and sneakers that were broken in but had been properly aired out after every use smelled, if not exactly good, then at least productive and useful and utilitarian and workmanlike and dignified by their hard service, they smelled sort of proud, in a sense, just like a hammer or a rake or a cane that has been used for years smells like what a humble integrity would smell like if integrity had a smell.

But used sneakers that had not been properly aired out in the mudroom or the basement or the sunroom or the garage did *not* smell good, they smelled *terrible*, they smelled foul and searing and loud, they smelled like rodents had died in them or wasps had conducted in them satanic ceremonies having to do with uric acid, and worst of all were the used and improperly aired sneakers of teenaged boys, for teenaged boys emit something horrifying through the skin of their enormous feet, like the poison arrow frogs and milk frogs and harlequin toads and cane toads of the American tropics, none of whom you would touch with a thousand-foot pole, if there was such a thing, with which you should not touch a teenaged boy's sneakers, either, trust me.

Nor did the players smell good. Let us be honest. They smelled terrible. Some of them had not washed their shirts or shorts or socks for eons, but simply left these ragged bedraggled fabrics to dry stiffly on balconies and porches and decks and garages, though they were *never washed or even rinsed before being hung to dry*, so that a battered old college shirt, for example, that had been drenched with sweat in the afternoon, was simply draped to dry on a dusty bicycle in the mudroom, and then *worn again the next day*, though it was stiff and smelled beyond any word we have yet invented for awful. Some guys did this for weeks at a time, and that is bad enough, but there were other guys, and every basketball player who ever played can still smell these other guys, who would wear that same shirt or shorts or sweats or socks *for months at a time*, until finally you could smell them coming two days before the game began, and you would foul them as hard as you could when they walked in the gym, on general principle, and you would be right and justified in this, and not alone, either.

On balance, though, the game smelled good, in most of its parts, from venues to instruments to accoutrements, and I have spent years trying to articulate the deep satisfying rich redolent foundations of the better smells of the game. At its best the game smelled like anticipation, and camaraderie, and freedom from quotidian concerns; it smelled like exercise, and grace, and creativity, and humor, and competition; finally, deepest, perhaps, it smelled like pleasure. Why do we so love the scent of a summer beach, an autumnal forest trail, a table laid with wonderful foodstuffs? Because, like basketball, they smell like probable pleasure; with the unforgettable exception of those fetid shirts and socks. How could a man possibly wear the same shirt and socks again and again and again for weeks or months at a time, and not be attacked by uncountable wasps with tiny buckets of uric acid? How could that be?

Getting the Nod

Yet another thing I loved about basketball was its endless series of silent signs and signals, its codes and languages, its gestures and intimations, such as:

The almost imperceptible nod your point guard gives you as you drift upcourt together, which means that he will drive hard to the basket and then whip the ball out to the corner where you had better be waiting with hands up and ready or else the ball will hit you in the face because he will deliver it at one hundred miles an hour and expect you to catch and shoot it in one smooth motion;

Or the nod your fellow defender gives you as you drift back on defense which means you will in about four seconds both leap at the ball handler to rattle him into a turnover;

Or the way your fellow forward wipes his wrist against his forehead as you both arrive in the lane which means let's switch sides and see if one of these fool defenders gets confused and loses his guy which means an easy basket;

Or the one of two plays indicated by the point guard's fist as he opens it like the flaring tail of a hawk, or closes it tight like a rock; or the way a player pats his chest with that ancient mea-culpa gesture meaning my fault, boys, my fault; or the quick pointing of a finger at the player who's just delivered you a lovely pass for a basket, a generous and gracious gesture, I've always thought, a graceful way to say thanks in a hurry; or the referee's pointing this way and that with flair and drama and panache, indicating which team now has possession; or the way a player occasionally raises his hand to acknowledge mournfully that yes, he committed the foul, he flouted the law, he incurred the infraction, it is he who was guilty of misdemeanor, and he says this publicly with his hand, in a gesture that even in the largest richest most accomplished players still seems gently boyish, as if the man's body, in the swiftness of the moment, recalls what it was taught to do when he was eight and ten and twelve years old, playing in the bantam league, the peewee league, the church league, the summer camp tournament, long ago and far away now, but his body remembers.

Or the curt nod from the coach, as he looks down the line of eager substitutes, each craning to catch his eye, each indicating with every fiber of his being that he's ready, coach, he's the one to put in now, he's itching to contribute, pick me pick me pick me, and the coach nods, and the chosen player leaps up and strips off his warm-up shirt and sprints to the scorer's table, where the scorer also nods, to indicate that he has noted the substitution.

The casual touching of hands in appreciation for fine plays; the way you occasionally shove your teammate toward the place on the floor he is supposed to be occupying but isn't quite yet; the drape of arms on shoulders during timeouts; the occasional wink as a player acknowledges to his teammates the fact that no, he hadn't the slightest intention of banking that shot in, and yes, it was utter and complete and ludicrous luck on his part, but we are not going to admit that to anyone other than us, are we boys?

In my memory it is the point guard who had the greatest array of signs and signals, gestures and intimations, and the most subtle and entertaining of these were mere flickers of the eyes; the quick glance up, meaning that if you cut hard and took off he would toss an alley-oop pass to catch your pedestrian defender by surprise; the quick glance to one side or another indicating where he wished you to carve out space to receive a pass; the direct annoyed stare, which from one terrific guard I played with meant No, I am not giving you the ball there, no matter how much you silently plead with me, or wave your hand in embarrassingly dramatic fashion, or glare back at me in some useless contest of wills, for *I* have the ball, and *I* decide where the ball goes, and if you do not move off that spot, no matter how much you love that spot and have told me so, and how little respect you have for your defender and have told me so, you will never get the ball again, am I making myself clear? And even I, the most selfish of players, would have to grin and abandon my spot; this grin too being, of course, a lovely silent signal.

Wild Impossible Shots

A Note

Some years ago I was living on an island off the Massachusetts coast with a dear friend of mine named Pete. We were both fanatic basketball players and tried to play every day if possible. There was no gym on the island so we played on a court near the beach whenever we could. This court was subject to the most astonishing blizzards and windstorms and hails of fallen leaves and vast banks of fog and occasionally hurtling ducks and once, interestingly, a bluefish about eighteen inches long. How the bluefish got onto the court was a mystery. Pete supposed that someone had placed it there, but I wondered if bluefish in general were more absorbed by basketball than anyone knew, or if this particular fish had a hoop jones that could be assuaged only by emerging from the sea and squirming onto the court. The fish was deceased. We thought about removing it but that seemed disrespectful somehow so we played around it.

That spring it snowed heavily all the way into May and then finally the weather broke and there was a thaw. By then we were stir-crazy and had not played ball for eight days and we could not bear the inaction any longer so we slogged down to the court by the beach. The court was a whole new landscape of snow hillocks so big and slushy that not even two crazy men could possibly play ball there, so we decided, in the way of intent idiots, to have a shooting contest. Just then the sun actually broke through the clouds, and something about the shocking light, so long absent and now so wonderfully flagrant, made us try one wild impossible shot after another. The thing with wild impossible shots is that every once in a while, one time in a hundred maybe, the shot drops cleanly and crisply and inarguably through the basket, and in my experience when this happens you get a jolt of such bubbling silly little-kid goofy hilarious joy that you caper and skip and duck-walk and crow and preen and make sharp staccato indecipherable howls and barks that make you laugh so hard your cheeks hurt.

And this happened. Pete tried this shot more than forty times: Toss it a mile high, watch it bounce crazily off the flat-topped pole at the corner of the fence, and soar above the basket, and glance off the backboard at exactly the right spot and angle so that it drops cleanly and crisply and inarguably through the basket, shaking off the dripping icicles that have taken root there over the last week, and plop down finally with a gentle sigh into the snow pile under the basket with the contented sound of a grizzled uncle on his third whiskey.

I counted the first twenty times Pete tried this shot, and then I started calling him names, and saying that we should get going, and offering up visions of steaming hot oyster chowder, and mulled wine, and hot whiskey toddies with lemon and honey, and almost certainly the Celtics playoff game against the Sixers was about to start, but he kept shooting, being intent on hitting this shot just once before we left the court, and I lost track of his attempts, but still I watched each additional attempt, because how ridiculously cool would it be if he actually *hit* that impossible shot, and then along about the fiftieth time, he did. It dropped right through the frozen net with a lovely tinkling chime, and Pete lost his mind and went capering around the court through the snow, and I laughed so hard my cheeks hurt for days, and then we retrieved the ball and went home and drank whiskey toddies and watched the Celts. They lost by eleven, though Kevin McHale had a terrific game that would have been a sin to miss (twenty-five points, seventeen rebounds, four blocks), but all in all we felt like it had been a victorious day, for reasons that are hard to articulate. But you understand.

Choosing Guys

A crucial but subtle aspect of playing pickup basketball, street ball, park ball, casual ball, ununiformed ball, rat-ball, unorganized ball, is the art of picking teammates from the general run of ruffians available; let us say that you and a friend have claimed a court, and have decided to run four on four, and one of you has done the requisite loud public inquiry as to who is up for a game, and a motley array of candidates has shuffled over from the other baskets, and you have flipped a coin for first pick, and now it is time for you and your friend to choose teammates from the gangly misdemeanors available. How is this done?

First rule: While you want desperately to take the tallest guy, do not do so, for he looks alluringly tall when he is standing there slack-jawed and gently drooling on himself, but as soon as he takes two steps you will see why his only virtue as a ballplayer is that he is tall, for if he can run up and down the court twice without breaking something, it will be a miracle, and this is before you even imagine him with a ball in his hands, a horrifying idea.

Second rule: Beware the guy with wristbands. Any guy with wristbands has an opinion of himself as a ballplayer that does not reflect reality and physics as we know them on this planet. Do not choose that guy. Let him infect the other team.

Third rule: Don't be afraid to choose the fat guy. Fat guys are often decent rebounders, they often set mammoth picks, they tend not to be arrogant and selfish, and at the very least they take up a lot of space. Also all fat guys are better off now because of Charles Barkley, who was inarguably and undeniably a fat guy, but a terrific ballplayer. It's unlikely that there will ever be another unbelievably great fat guy like Charles Barkley, but you never know.

Fourth rule: Don't be afraid to pick a geeky guy with zits or spectacles or a ridiculous bandanna wrapped around a head shaped like a mutant pineapple. Geeky guys are often startlingly good ballplayers and they have a useful chippy edge to them because they get their revenge on court for all the indignities inflicted on them off court. One of the best rat-ball players I ever saw in my life was the geekiest guy ever, with zits and spectacles and oily flaccid unkempt hair and worn low-cut sneakers, and that guy hammered everyone who covered him, without exception and without a shred of mercy. He was amazing to watch. He was the Geek Jesus on the basketball court.

Fifth rule: Beware muscleheads, and guys who have deliberately taken off their shirts to show off their toned torsos, and guys who chatter, and guys with shiny jerseys with the names of former or current professional ballplayers, because these last guys especially will try to show that they can play like Kobe or Bird or Michael, and they cannot, and the gap between Try and Cannot is incomprehensibly vast, and you will lose by eight with any of these guys, trust me.

Sixth rule: Brothers and friends are generally good choices, because you know what you are getting. Little brothers are the best choices of all because often they have the same useful chippy edge that geeky guys have. The best of all choices like this is a geeky younger brother, if you have one, or four.

Seventh rule: When in doubt, pretend that you have a sudden leg cramp and have to stretch it out, and tell all the candidates to shoot around for a minute while you work the knot out, thanks, guys, and then as you fake stretching out the cramp, watch them dribble and shoot, and then choose the guy who stands under the basket and whips passes back out to the shooters. That guy has his ego in check and he can pass. Take him first, and then take the geeky guy who calmly hit three corner jumpers in a row and looked like it wasn't a shock to him that he hit them. Then take a kid brother, ideally one with some meat on him, or a fat guy, and start the game, because there are guys waiting, and you can't overthink this, man. Let's *go*.

Backspin

My older brother was a mediocre basketball player, but he was my older brother, and a swift and omnivorous learner all his life. So it was that during the summer I was nine years old, and intent on making my very first basketball team that fall, he taught me how to shoot a basketball, though he was a mediocre basketball player himself then and later, and could not score unless he was so close to the basket that a prom chaperone would have stormed onto the dance floor and separated them forcibly and sent my brother to the men's room to cool off and remember that there are such things as propriety and dignified behavior in the public arena.

At the age of nine a shooter is concerned primarily with hoist; you want to get the ball, which is the size of a dwarf planet, up into the air, and vaguely toward the basket, so most players at that age fling it up underhand with both hands, or sling it up wildly with one hand as if throwing an uppercut, or attempt a two-handed set shot that makes the nearest grandfather start telling stories about drinking beer and shooting snipe with Bob Cousy. My older brother, though, had studied the craft of shooting, and concluded that the only proper way to shoot was with one hand cupped under the ball and the other gently guiding it; and the shot had to be released not from your belt buckle, but from high over your crew-cut head, with a serious flick of the wrist to impart backspin, which softened your shot and gave it, he estimated, an extra twenty percent chance of bouncing around and in.

This all sounded great in theory, but the fact of the matter was that I was a brief young man at age nine, and not yet sinewy enough to shoot with proper form and actually reach the basket, so that when I shot with proper form, the ball arose weakly, like a wounded snipe making a last effort to escape Bob Cousy, and then fell feebly to the ground, long before the basket was aware that anything was due to arrive. To me the solution to this problem was to go back to slinging the thing wildly into the air and hoping for the best, but my older brother was an intent and inarguable young man, decisive and disciplined and also much bigger and stronger than me; and so I spent every day that summer taking one hundred shots minimum with the correct form, beginning with shots from three feet away, and then, as the weeks went by, backing up slowly to five feet and finally, in August, ten feet, which is where I stopped, because my brother went off to college.

The day after he went to college was a somber day in our house and even on our street, as all our neighbors knew that he was gone, and were solicitous about his absence; I remember one mother bringing over lasagna and cookies, as you would when a neighbor was in the hospital, or there had been a death in the family. It was quiet in the kitchen, at the table, in his echoing empty room downstairs; we all wandered around silently, feeling his absence more, I think, than we had ever felt his presence; you take someone's presence for granted, and only notice the weight of it when it is missing, as you only notice a dent in the couch after the cause of the dent is gone.

I went out to the hoop and took my one hundred shots, first from three feet, and then from five, and then from ten. I counted by tens to be sure I shot my one hundred shots. Then, feeling wobbly and near tears, I took another eighteen shots, because he was eighteen years old, and then I went to my room for a while and practiced the proper way to flick your wrist as you release your shot, so as to impart backspin, which softened your shot, and gave it, my brother estimated, an extra twenty percent chance of it going in. Of course he had studied the matter closely, and if *he* said it was an extra twenty percent chance, believe me, it was exactly twenty percent.

A Net Note

Mesh nets, steel nets, half nets, nylon nets, no nets . . . bringing your own net to the park and putting it on the basket by jumping up and hanging for an instant on the back of the rim while your sturdiest brother or buddy set your feet on his shoulders and started moaning melodramatically about your vast weight and fumbling fingers and *Man hurry up I am about to drop you* and just as he groans piteously for the third time you get that last recalcitrant loop done and you drop to the court and say *Let's go let's go* . . .

And hitting jump shots so cleanly from either baseline that the net got hung up on the rim which was a very cool thing to see and sort of a triumphant thing when you think about it in that the net acknowledged and saluted your accuracy, and once again someone would have to hop up and yank the net down or flip the ball back up through the basket from underneath while you and your teammates drifted back on defense happy for a few seconds of rest . . .

And the deeply grindingly frustrating experience of playing on a basket with *no* net, which is a curiously unfulfilling experience, because when someone hits a shot you all miss the ever-so-slight riffle and ripple and hiss and sigh of the net as the ball falls through—as lovely and subtle and productive and satisfying a sound as there is the game of basketball, and that's a fact. Not to mention that every single time you ever played a game on a basket with no net, or even worse a court missing *both* nets, without fail someone would miss a shot and claim it went through cleanly, or someone would drill a shot cleanly and someone else would adamantly and vehemently dispute the fact that it went through the rim at *all*, and this would

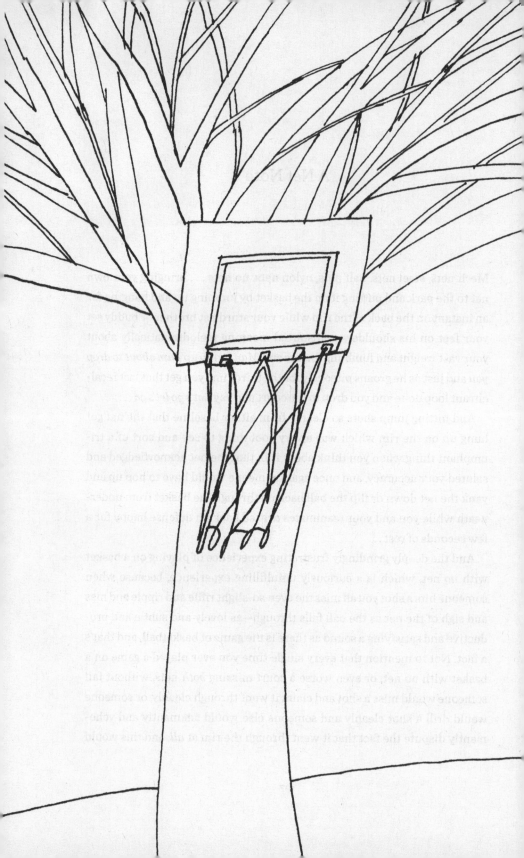

lead to arguing and cursing and bitterness and disputation, all of which is unpleasant and interferes with the pace and pleasure of the game and sometimes even led to fisticuffs and grim hard fouls long after the shot had been missed, or made, for which I blame the egregious absence of nets.

The net announces a successful shot; the net is a flag, a pennant, a banner, a statement, a form of applause; the net can even assist you sometimes, such as when you have your defender on your shoulder, and you go up for a reverse layup, and he goes up with you, and he gets his hand tangled in the net, which is amusing if it is a string net, and awful if it is a steel net; I always half-expected to someday see a finger dangling in a steel net, but I never have, yet.

Sometimes the nets would be half on and half off the rim, so that sometimes an accurate shot swished, but sometimes it made no sound at all and bred arguments as to whether you had nailed or airballed your shot; sometimes nets would be strung so tightly and weirdly that a shot would actually no-kidding bounce *out* of the basket, as if rejected by the gods of the underworld; sometimes nets would finally just quit altogether when a shot fell through, so that the ball, which would normally fall directly below the basket, would squirt off in a strange direction, toward the Mysterious East, or Foster Avenue, or Brighton Beach.

I have seen handmade nets made of packaging twine, and lengths of laundry line, and even the same riddled plastic of which wiffle balls are made. In Queens once I saw a net made simply of burlap sacking, attached to the rim by duct tape. I possess and savor a photograph of Doctor James Naismith's famous peach basket, through which the very first game of basketball was played, in Massachusetts, on December 21, 1891; the doctor cut the bottom out of the basket and hung it on the wall, and a few minutes later one of the players scored, which not only was the first basket ever, but the first time a net, so to speak, felt the burl of the ball—a momentous moment, yes?

The Interior Calculus of Ball

A kid asked me the other day *When were you happiest as a basketball player?*

And weirdly enough what came first to mind was not my highest-scoring game, or the game where I wasn't completely humiliated against college and slumming pro players, or the myriad joys of several years of almost-daily games with my friends who were excellent players, or the hilarity of ceremonial games before weddings, or the time my college dorm team beat Joe Montana's dorm team, or the many thrilling moving piercing delighted inarticulately cool times I coached my sons' basketball teams, or watched my daughter cause chaos and mayhem with her lightning-quick hands on defense although she could not score if you locked her in the gym for a week;

No, the first thing that popped to mind, strangely, was the summer after I'd had ankle surgery. I remember getting the awkward uncomfortable cast off, and being appalled at the feeble pale dead twig where my left foot used to be. I remember walking gingerly along the beach, nervously trying to distinguish between mere soreness and actual pain. I remember a doctor telling me that I should try to spell the alphabet with my foot all day long so as to stretch and exercise it while at work. I remember beginning to jog gently and fearfully along the beach, and then a few days later beginning to run, and then a few days later beginning to sprint, and then setting up an obsessive maniacal sprint-walk-sprint schedule to be executed every evening and twice a day on weekends. I remember putting my sneakers on for the first time in months, and spending an inordinate amount of time tightening the laces just so, and picking up my old worn shining beloved ball, and walking out onto a court, and stretching before shooting, and being thrilled and afraid. I remember a green heron glaring at me from a pine tree. I remember walking around the court for a long time, dribbling with one hand and then the other, and then behind my back and between my legs, to get the rhythm back, the thoughtless ease, the unconscious knowledge of body and ball and distance and height and angle and probability; the interior calculus of ball, the way everything fits without effort when things are right.

And then the drills—layups with either hand to get loose, and then ten hooks with one hand and ten with the other, and then five foul shots, and then ten jumpers from one corner and ten from the other, and five foul shots, and then long set shots from oblique angles, and five foul shots, and then stutter-step drives to the basket, and reverse layups, and ten foul shots, and then one or more long jumpers from the top of the key, as many as it takes to hit one last one cleanly, and then ten laps around the court, and then home for sit-ups and push-ups and the longest hottest shower possible. Repeat the next day, and the next, for a week, and then two, and then the rest of the summer, and by the time the season began I was back in form; and while I was never the same headlong player I had been before, I found that I was a much better shooter, in large part, I think, because I had been forced to slow down, and accept the gift of space in which to shoot, rather than trying constantly to force space, to create space by hurtling into what I thought was an opening, although often it was instead a startled and displeased opponent.

Slowly, as the years passed, I came to realize how my interior calculus had been reordered by that injury, and the lessons it forced on me; but also I began to understand how happy I had been, working my way back. It was just me and the ball and the basket and that heron, day after day, easy and mindless and sweating and delighted. It still sounds odd to say that the happiest I ever was in basketball was after I had lost it for months, but that's true, and there are days even now when I close my eyes and feel every atom of that place and time; I can even, if I look hard, still see that hunched little heron glaring at me from his pine tree.

A Series of Humiliating Epiphanies

Another great thing about being a total basketball fanatic as a young man was that the game was a steady series of humiliating epiphanies; basketball is a wonderfully blunt and honest and inarguable sport, in which the fact that one player is better than another is an undebatable state of affairs, not subject to judicial review or appeal. When you play a guy who is better than you, and you get hammered, the cold fact of the matter is that you got hammered, and he's better, and you either work maniacally to rise to his level, or you play down, and spend your time happily hammering lesser players— the latter an undeniable pleasure, albeit a shallow and finally an empty one, in my experience; plus the youngest brother I hammered so happily when he was small grew into a large and terrific player who savored killing the king again and again, occasionally paying off the ancient debt with an elbow like an axe.

When young, despite my thick spectacles, I was a good ballplayer, for I had an older brother who'd taught me to shoot, and I loved the game, and loved repetitive mindless drills, and did every sort of drill on my own for what must have been thousands of hours in toto—dribbling through thickets of traffic cones and folding chairs, playing endless games of playground and street ball with friends and classmates, running for miles and miles along streets and avenues and the perimeters of parks and schoolyards, for even then I knew somehow that being tireless, and being able to dribble confidently and unconsciously, would be great assets; and so they were, and I made my first teams, and adored my uniform jerseys, and kept them folded carefully in a drawer that no brother was allowed to open, for therein resided hallowed things of green and gold that only ten boys in this world could wear.

But as I grew older I encountered better ballplayers by the day, sometimes by the hour, occasionally in the space of a few minutes, as a game began, and I realized all too soon that I would do well merely to hold my own and not embarrass myself in such august company; and while this was initially dismaying in the extreme, I soon came to appreciate the naked honesty of this phenomenon; the game itself was clear and sharp about itself, it was a game in which natter and chatter held no weight; a man might consider himself a fine player, and have heretofore proven himself a fine player on this court and that, but when he found himself in a game with better players, no amount of ego or opinion or past glitter could save him from the realization that there were whole clans and tribes of finer players than he; and it is another thing I love about basketball that even the very best players in the world come to this same epiphany, and all but two or three, perhaps, know very well, deep in their hearts, that there are better players above them, if not by much.

I came to grips with this, I made my peace with it, I came to appreciate and even love it, when I was still in my early teens; and there are many days now when I think what might be construed as a hard lesson was actually a great thing in the making of a man. To be forced to be honest about yourself is refreshing even when it is humiliating. Perhaps that which forces us to achieve humility is a gift, though we do not see it as such without strenuous effort; but when we do, we are far better for the knowledge that we are only who we are. And isn't that an eloquent and articulate illustration of whatever it is we mean when we say *maturity*? We spend so very much time in the theater of the self, the performance of who we wish to be, the illusion of who we think we are, that a jolt of cold humiliation is medicinal; if we did not swallow it occasionally, we would be only that which we pretend to be, which is another way to say *hell*.

Cuts and Spins and Whirls

A Note

There are eight million ways to cut and spin and reverse and whirl in basketball, and this morning my mind reminds my body of how we used to be, flying toward the basket with only one defender backpedaling, and you take a step to your right, his left, so that he thinks you are about to drop your shoulder to drive past him to his off hand, but the instant he commits to cutting you off to that side you spin back the other way, cupping the ball for a split second before leaving it in the air for your left hand to pick up, and then as the defender staggers to get back into the picture you can, if you can actually shoot with your off hand, just drive smoothly and casually and easily to the basket, or you can do as I had to do, which is awkwardly switch back to my good hand and try to lay the thing in hurriedly before being hammered by the embarrassed defender, who, if you conducted your spin move correctly, appears to have leapt out of the way as you approached, which makes him subject to the razzing of his teammates, and no player likes being razzed, much.

And there is the backdoor cut, which entails a lazy step or two in one direction and then a hard fast cut straight to the basket, which ideally leads to a perfect little thread-the-needle pass from your attentive point guard for an easy basket; and there is the drift cut, during which you drift one way lazily behind a screen and then cut back hard the other way, leaving your defender crammed up against the adamant pick, while you accept another crisp pass from your astute point guard, and hit a short jumper; and then there is the jump cut, which an alert ball handler will pull off once a game, which is beautiful and startling to watch, as two defenders close in on the

ball handler, cutting off his passing and driving lanes, so that you and everyone else on the floor are sure there is about to be a turnover or a foul or both,
when suddenly the ball handler, who has intelligently kept up his dribble,
just miraculously hops through the defenders, popping through the small
space among their legs and arms and grasping greedy hands, and away he
goes, as the defenders look around for the guy who was inarguably trapped
between them one second ago. Once in a summer-league game I was close
enough to this play to see the expression on the faces of the defenders just
after our perspicacious point guard had escaped their trap, and you never
saw two guys who looked more like they had misplaced the car keys they
had *just had in their hands*, how could you conceivably lose the keys you
just had in your hand? How? I laughed so hard I had to go sit down.

Then there is the reverse pivot, in which you receive the ball from your
brilliant point guard and then, instead of spinning with your back to the
defender, you spin frontwise, right into him, as it were, which startles him,
and you take advantage of his being startled by immediately sailing past
him to the basket; and then there is a complete pivot, during which you
plant one foot and then whirl all the way around and back to where you
started, a move that only works against over-eager defenders, who try to
anticipate what move you are making before you make it, which allows
you to simply reverse away from whatever poor decision they made, and
score; and then there is the drag cut, which also works best against an
eager defender, the kind of detestable guy who follows you everywhere,
which can be hugely annoying, but which turns out to be delightful when
you make a drag cut, because he has followed you here and there around
picks and behind screens, he has picked you up to defend at half court, he is
intent and glaring and clearly believes that he is a terrific defender who is
going to shut you down, and with mounting pleasure you notice that two of
your teammates have seen what kind of tool this guy is, and they are setting
up for you to do the drag cut, which entails you drifting aimlessly out by the
top of the key, trailed maniacally by your grim hair shirt of a defender, and
then you cut straight down the lane as hard as you can, followed by your
avid defender, who is a half step behind because he did not anticipate that
you would cut so hard and fast down the lane, and as you whiz through your
two teammates, and receive a lovely little drop pass from your generous

and handsome point guard, and score easily, your teammates slam the door behind you, and your defender crashes into them, and after the game you and your teammates laugh yourselves silly about this play, which is also called an *elevator door*, and a *stack*, but we called it a *drag cut*, because you dragged your defender down the lane to his doom, and it felt great, although the defender fouled you extra hard the next time he fouled you.

There are many other lovely and graceful and brutal movements in the game of basketball, but we had better stop here, because my stomach hurts from laughing at the two guys looking for the car keys they just had in their hands *one second ago*, how could you possibly lose your keys that fast?

Being Beaver Smith

One time I went down to the local basketball court to shoot around and a few minutes later a local college basketball star showed up with a friend. The friend was competent but not anywhere near the class of the star. We all shot around for a few minutes and I watched the star without watching, you know? He was tall and muscled but what really struck me was the absolute deft easy graceful swift unhurried efficiency of his movements; he never hurried or seemed to make the slightest effort, but his shots dropped cleanly, he rose lightly to dunk, his passes were crisp and perfectly timed. At one point he practiced spins and pivots for a moment, and his friend and I stood and gaped at the sculptural economy of motion. Sometimes, if you are lucky and attentive, you see athletes who are born to their sports, who almost encapsulate or incarnate their sports, and this was most certainly the case with William Smith, better known as Beaver, of Saint John's University in the Borough of Queens, New York City. Beaver had been a high-school star, and Beaver was now a college star, and Beaver would be chosen by the Knicks a year later in the professional draft, but for the moment Beaver was on the court with two far lesser players, and he was itching to get a good workout, but we were short a guy. We were about to reluctantly play one on two full court when suddenly a boy of about ten walked by, and Beaver recruited him for our game.

So we played two on two full court, Beaver and the kid against me and Beaver's friend, who never did tell me his name; in the way of all pickup ballplayers ever he called me Hey and I called him Hey when we needed to communicate. We huddled for a moment before we began and decided to double Beaver eternally, rather than waste time respecting a ten-year-old. If we played ferocious defense on Beaver we might bother him sufficiently that he would not score every time down; on offense we would just run hell for leather and hope to outscore Beaver before he shifted into an unstoppable gear.

As I remember we didn't exactly slow Beaver, but we bothered him into a couple of turnovers, and Hey and I ran like rabbits, taking no mercy whatsoever on the kid, as was right and proper—never give an opponent a break, never play down to an opponent; it's finally disrespectful, and it's bad for your own game; the unspoken rule is that if you are on a court you are ready to play, whether you are ten years old or have a broken finger or whatever, and if you get hammered, well, you got hammered, and someday you will hammer someone else in your turn; basketball is a grimly ruthless sport; the better players hammer the lesser players, and thus the lesser players learn how to be better, sometimes.

We were playing to fifteen baskets, win by one, and Beaver and the kid had the ball, one basket to win, and I can still see the play out of the corner of my eye; Hey and I attacked Beaver, trying to jostle the ball loose, but Beaver turns slightly and delivers the most beautiful sharp crisp pass, right between us, to the kid cutting to the basket. The kid catches it, a little off-stride, and goes up for a layup, but he misses badly, and Hey gets the rebound and sails away for the basket that wins the game. I have followed him by instinct, in case he misses, so I am at the far end of the court when I turn and see the kid in tears and Beaver standing over him like a tree. Hey wanders off for water but I walk down to shake hands and hear Beaver telling the kid that he'd made exactly the right cut, at exactly the right instant, and he, Beaver, was knocked out by the cut, *he'd* never have made that cut when *he* was ten years old, and besides my pass was too heavy, I should have feathered it, man. My bad, little brother, he says to the kid. You ready to run again? This time we smoke these jokers good. I'll play better this time, I promise.

We played again and they smoked us and I had to get home and it was only when I was almost home that I suddenly realized the most graceful thing I had seen that day was not Beaver Smith playing basketball but

Beaver Smith being Beaver Smith. Maybe if we are lucky and attentive all the small-not-small moments of grace we ever witnessed or performed or were graced by add up finally into something that goes a long way to defining whatever it is we mean when we say the words *character*, or *blessing*, or *humility*, or *love*. Maybe.

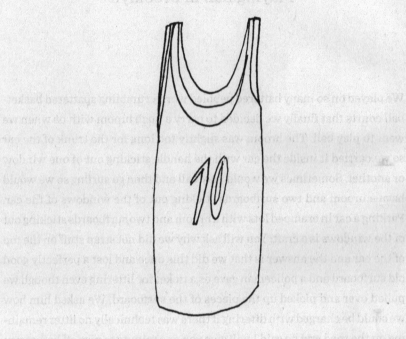

Playing Ball in Brooklyn

We played on so many battered pebbled worn crumbling spattered basketball courts that finally we decided to carry a push broom with us when we went to play ball. The broom was slightly too long for the trunk of the car so we carried it inside the car with the handle sticking out of one window or another. Sometimes we would play ball and then go surfing so we would have a broom and two surfboards sticking out of the windows of the car. Parking a car in cramped lots with a broom and two surfboards sticking out of the windows is a craft. You will ask why we did not strap stuff on the top of the car and the answer is that we did this once and lost a perfectly good old surfboard and a policeman gave us a ticket for littering even though we pulled over and picked up the pieces of the surfboard. We asked him how we could be charged with littering if there was technically no litter remaining on the road and he said I will give you one minute to piss off before you incur another ticket. I remember that he used the word *incur*, which is a rare and lovely word.

We played on so many courts that needed to be swept before you could play that we could identify detritus by borough. In Brooklyn it was broken glass, in the Bronx it was crumbled chunks of asphalt and brick, in Queens it was sand and dirt and pigeon feathers, in Manhattan it was disgusting things that I don't want to talk about, and we never went to Staten Island, because who wants to go all the way through Brooklyn to get to Staten Island? If you have to get to Staten Island by going through Brooklyn, and Brooklyn has basketball courts, wouldn't you just play ball in Brooklyn? Of course you would. Which is why we never did get to Staten Island. Even today when people find out I am from New York they will say *Oh, the Five Boroughs*, and I always think, five?

It seemed to us that Brooklyn also was the windiest borough, especially down by the beach, so that even if you waited to sweep the court until you had all stretched, and shot around to get loose, and chosen teams, the court was somehow glinting with glass again even before you finished the first game. This was manifestly impossible, except that we were in Brooklyn, and all sorts of things were possible in Brooklyn that were not possible anywhere else, like a guy moving into his wife's tomb on Bushwick Avenue and living there for ten years, and another guy making wings out of canvas sails and flying off the Brooklyn Bridge, and twenty elephants walking over the bridge one day, all of which happened, because why? Because Brooklyn, that's why.

To get to Brooklyn from our house you would take the Belt Parkway to Atlantic Avenue, passing the Aqueduct horse-racing track along the way, and Evergreens Cemetery, where the guy lived for ten years with his dead wife, and once on Atlantic Avenue we would head north or south depending on whim and the wind. One time we were driving with a new guy we had not played with much and he didn't know the drill and he said hey let's hit Staten Island and find a game and we said, gently, that to get to the Verrazano Bridge you had to go all the way through Flatbush to Bensonhurst, and why would you do that unless you owed somebody money or something, but his question made us all envision the sea for a moment, so that day we went south and played all afternoon at Brighton Beach, where the courts were covered with sand and there were significant drifts of sand on one side of the court. When you stood out of bounds on that side of the court your sneakers left prints in the sand, which is not a sentence you see every day. But we do today, because why? Because Brooklyn, that's why.

A Note on Redolence

Everybody who's ever played basketball on a regular or OK let's be honest obsessive and compulsive and maniacal basis has favorite shirts and shorts and socks as well as sneakers, and while ballplayers' adoration for their favorite sneakers, for sneakers that miraculously make you a better shooter and a better leaper, for sneakers that have victories stitched into them somehow by mystical unknown geniuses in the sneaker factory, is fairly well documented, ballplayers' common absorption with favorite shirts and etc. is not, so let us go there, holding our noses against the incredible eye-watering stench of that pitiful softball shirt, that pair of cutoff sweats, that ancient pair of shorts you stole from the Young Men's Christian Association some years ago and were always going to return but you never actually did and finally they just dissolved one day with a small plaintive moan.

Every one of us has played against a guy wearing a shirt unwashed since Nixon was a child. As soon as he walks onto the court everyone knows beyond the shadow of a doubt that the guy with the Fordham shirt has not washed it *ever*, even though he's worn it twice a week, and soaked it through with sweat each time, and then gone home and *hung it up on the railing of the back porch*, and *left it there to harden*, until he's just grabbed it off the railing *and put it on again to go play ball*.

All sorts of questions arise at this point. Did he never notice that his shirt is now more concrete art than cotton cloth? Was he not horrified by the violent stench, and did he not notice the asphyxiated birds on the porch? Did he not think, while struggling to get the shirt on, that shirts usually don't fight back when you don them, and perhaps he ought to wash it annually, or choose another shirt, or hit himself with a rock fifty times in expiation for idiocy?

Unwashed socks are even worse, but they are farther away from your nose, and partially sheathed by sneakers; shorts and sweatpants can reek awfully, but at least you are rarely in the position of touching such vulgar things; but shirts—shirts have to be grabbed, shirts are right under your nose, shirts can carry a shocking amount of sweat, and it is all too clear, to everyone on the court, within the first few baskets, who has blessedly washed his shirt, or at least soaked it in the sink and wrung it out before hanging it on the porch, and who has most definitely not done this simple and sensible thing since Warren Gamaliel Harding was president.

Do we deliberately foul such a guy sometimes? We do. Do we occasionally foul such a guy harder than necessary? We do. Do we occasionally make a concerted effort, without consulting each other verbally, to tear and rip such a shirt, such that the shirt became a flapping useless rag, and the wearer has to borrow another shirt? We do. Are we ourselves guilty of owning such shirts? We are. I myself had a shirt that I used to hang on the railing of the back stairs on an ancient Boston three-flat, and soon none of my roommates would use those stairs any more, and burglars and meter readers wouldn't use the stairs, and one time when a guy stored an extra mattress on those stairs for two weeks and then went to get the mattress he had to throw the mattress away and he was *very* bitter about this for a surprisingly long time. Finally one evening when I opened the door to the back stairs to get the shirt for a summer league game there was a low savage growl from the shadows and I closed the door hurriedly and got another shirt and then moved as far away as possible. To this day I sometimes wonder what happened to that shirt, but there are many things for which there are no answers, and a surprising number of things about which you probably shouldn't even ask the question.

The Common Cold of Basketball Injuries

Of all the many injuries you can and will incur on a basketball court, if you play long and hard and headlong enough, there are the little annoying nagging ones, like sprained fingers and stubbed toes and sore shoulders from crashing into guys as big as battleships; and then there are the weird ones, like long jagged scratches from guys who should really trim their fingernails more than once a decade just on general principle; and there are the occasional unusual but painful ones, like cracking your head against another guy's head when you both scramble for a loose ball, or banging your head against the court as you fall, or banging your head against the stanchion as you turn to watch your shot drop through the net; and there are the weird but sort of amusing if it's not you injuries like when a guy gets a finger stuck in the net or he punches the wire fence and the fence grabs his thumb and won't give it back; or the really odd injuries, like the time we were playing at Jacob Riis Park in Queens and a gull dove on a guy's tuna sandwich and the guy dove to save his sandwich and the gull nailed him in his right shoulder so hard that the guy had to shoot lefty the rest of the day, although he did save his sandwich.

Then there are the injuries no one likes to talk about, like awful concussions, and broken arms and legs, and shredded knees, and shattered elbows, and cracked vertebrae, and getting poked in the eye so bad that there's a *lot* of blood, but let's not talk about those.

Then there are the injuries that every player gets eventually, the pulled groin and pulled hamstring and shin splints and broken nose; and then, finally, there is the lingua franca of basketball injuries, the common cold of basketball injuries, the one every single player male or female or both or neither gets eventually, and gets more than once, and knows all too well, knows the instant flashing stabbing pain and the scream of frustration as you know without the shadow of a doubt that yes, you have, unbelievably, for the twentieth time, even though you taped your ankles so assiduously that a mummy would be proud, sprained your ankle yet again, and this time it's bad.

You stepped on a guy's foot and went down howling. You came down from a rebounding scrum and landed awkwardly. You did something as innocent and stupid as slipping on a pebble or a gleam of sweat on the floor from where the guy dove for his tuna sandwich. No matter what the cause, you limp off, cursing with all your might, and you sit down and peel off your sock and sneaker and there is exactly the sight you never wanted to see again—a rising lump like a golf ball on your ankle, and the first faint hue of the parade of colors you know all too well—a lurid surly yellow, a dark brooding blue, an snarling furious red, even sometimes some weird sickly venomous orange that is so unhealthy a color that you cover it with a brother's bandanna.

You limp to the park office and ask for ice, which they do not have. You get a ride home in sweaty teeth-grinding silence. You shower gingerly and then you ice that thing all day and night for three days, hoping against hope that it's minor, and maybe you can start shooting on the fourth day, but it's *not* minor, damn it, and it's another whole week before you are safely back on the court, and even then you are a little leery and neurotic and paranoid, because the last thing you want is to tweak it again, which happens about every fifth time, and is so deeply frustrating that I cannot find words for the feeling, and would prefer to stop here, and think happily of all the games when we did *not* sprain our ankles. There were far more of those than there were of the other kind, which was a blessing, when you think about it, which we didn't then, but do now.

An Entertaining Journey
through the Lane

Among the many puzzles and conundrums to be solved on a basketball court, when you have the ball, and there are various grim defenders
between you and the glory of an easy basket, is getting safely and swiftly
into the lane, past not only your specific defender, but also sometimes his
positional partner, if they are playing a zone, or if the partner is that sort of
detestable and unlikable soul who actually likes to play help defense and is
good at it, too.

Let us assume that this is the case, and as you cross half court with the
ball and greedy intent, you are immediately confronted, very nearly chest
to chest and nose to nose, with Defender One, who had something like gar-
lic shrimp for lunch, and was probably just dumped by his girlfriend this
morning, because he is unfriendly, and disrespectful of personal space
issues, and pushy, and muttering vulgar remarks about how he is going to
shut you down, and etc. in that vein, and while usually you would elbow
him sharply in the neck and proceed happily to the basket, today you are
screwed, because the referee is six feet away and watching like a hawk, and,
lo and behold, here comes the eager other guard like a headlong puppy.

Choices must be made. You could pass the ball out of this closing trap,
but that would be sensible and generous and selfless, and where is the fun
in that? You could back up and reconsider and reconnoiter, but that would
be safe and cautious, and where is the fun in that? So you do one of several
things: (a) hoist up a shot right quick, while pretending to be fouled; (b) try
a swift crossover dribble in hopes that the guards will crash into each other
and give you a sliver of space; or (c) try the almost-impossible slick leap

between them, in which you cup the ball for an instant and actually jump through the vanishing hole between the defenders. This is the highest-risk move possible, because you have to pop through the closing door in a split second, and carry the ball with you, even as the referee is looking for exactly that venial sin, but when someone pulls it off it's a wonderful thing, as if he just vanished and then miraculously reappeared, still dribbling, *behind* the confused defenders, so you try that, because it's ridiculous and cool, and miraculously it works, and now you are once again screwed, because here, eight feet tall with a beard and prison tattoos, is the opposing center, who is annoyed that he has to deal with a miniscule guard, in exactly the same way that eagles look aggrieved when being badgered by hummingbirds, which I have seen, and which never fails to make me laugh.

Again choices must be made. You can (a) flip the ball up as hurriedly as possible and hope for the best, (b) pass to any of the several teammates who by now are so open they crave company and human conversation, (c) actually do as my friend Billy used to do and drive right *at* the center and put your knee in his chest and climb him for a better shot, or (d) lean back a little, making him think that you are taking a fall-away shot, which is exactly what he wants, because then he can extend his full gargantuanity to block the shot, but instead you drive right past him and flip up a layup before he realizes what has happened. Most centers, to be wholly honest here, have a reaction time of about four months, but still, better safe than sorry.

You might miss that little flip shot; you might have it hammered into your face by a late-arriving forward; you might be fouled by all three of the angry defenders you have managed to evade; but then again you might hit the shot, and even if you miss it you have had an entertaining journey through the lane. And fun, it seems to me, is where it's at. Aren't games supposed to be fun? And what could be more fun than evading three defenders, failing to pass to three open teammates, causing your coach to swallow his cigar in gargled perplexity, and *almost* hitting a *very* difficult shot? Not much, I think. Not so much.

My College Basketball Career

I had a high opinion of myself as a basketball player when I was seventeen, but I can vividly remember the hour when my opinion was adjusted gently down toward reality as we know it on Earth. This was in an old gymnasium in Indiana. I had arrived early to college, being a shy freshman eager to get a handle on pattern before the rest of the students arrived, and I had dribbled my worn shining basketball down to the old gym, and meticulously taped my ankles, and carefully stretched my hamstrings, and gone through my well-worn practice drill (ten shots from each corner, ten from the key, ten from each wing, finish with ten hooks in the lane, twice up and down the court dribbling with each hand to get loose and find any dead spots in the floor), and then got drawn into a pickup game, and it was about ten minutes into this game that I went from being a guy with a high opinion of himself as a ballplayer to a guy who understood that there were players like me and then there were much, much better players, like the guy on my team who was just vacuuming all available rebounds and muscling the ball smoothly back into the basket, and the tall blond guy on the other team who was hitting shots from every conceivable angle and distance, no matter who was covering him or how many guys were covering him.

This second guy was the tallest guy on the other team, but for some reason he stayed out on the perimeter the whole game, defending our team's quicksilver point guard, and defending him stiflingly well, too, despite being easily six inches taller and twenty pounds heavier. You would think a taller broader guy would have trouble covering a slippery bolt of light like our point guard but I watched as the bigger guy calculated angles, cut

118

off driving lanes, slid through and over picks with deft footwork, and never let his man get more than a couple of feet away, so that the smaller man never could quite get enough room for a confident shot. I was impressed, but that was nothing compared to how impressed I was with the guy on my team who was snatching very nearly every rebound, and boxing out two guys at once in the mosh pit under the basket, and pulling up occasionally for short jump shots, each of which dropped cleanly through the exact center of the rim. This guy was all of six foot three, and while he was solid he was by no means especially muscled, but guys bounced off him when there were collisions and contests, and when he established position he owned that position pretty much as if it had been in his family for generations and he had the trust deed framed over the fireplace. But what really impressed me wasn't the startling number of rebounds, or the steady accumulation of baskets, or the way he didn't seem to be working overly hard on defense and yet his man was not scoring hardly at all; it was the utterly smooth easy calm patient grace with which he was dominating the game. Each motion was deft but not dramatic; he never flailed or seemed to be striving; he never showed any strain that I noticed; and yet he was always in the right place, always made the right play, and never said a word.

I should say at this juncture that I was playing as hard and well as I possibly could, and I was young and strong and fit and had been playing hours every day all summer, so I was pretty much at the peak of my ability, and while I was holding my own against the rest of the players on the floor, I was so ridiculously outclassed by these other two guys that I was, to be honest, shocked. I had played against terrific ballplayers before, in parks and playgrounds in New York, but this was a whole new order of terrific, and I was a little rattled.

We played for a solid hour, best three of five games to fifteen, and my team won, because no one in the gym could stop the rebounding machine on my team, not even the tall blond guy on the other team, who switched onto him for the fifth and deciding game. Afterward we all shook hands, and the tall blond guy turned out to be the captain of the college team, and the rebounding machine on my team turned out to be an All-American who would go on to a long and glittering professional career: Adrian Dantley.

I did not go on to a long and glittering career as a ballplayer, though no one ever loved the game more than I did; and part of the reason I love it so, I think now, is because it is an honest and forthright game, in which judges and referees are not really necessary, for when a guy is a lot better than you are, you know it and he knows it, and nothing need be said, and there is some blunt straightforward admirable integrity about this that says something subtle and true about the sport, and about those who play it. In a real sense I was a better player after that hour, for I knew myself better; and probably I was a better man, having been humbled; humility, as you and I know, is never savory, but it is always nutritious.

Who Was the Best Player
You Ever Played Against?

A small boy asks me that question this morning, and I am about to say Joe Montana, who was an unbe*liev*able basketball player before he went on to some notoriety in football, or Adrian Dantley, who is in the Basketball Hall of Fame, or Michael Adams, who was an NBA all-star and the quickest jitterbuggiest lightning bolt of a guy I ever saw, but of my mouth comes the name Kevin Green, and the kid looks at me confusedly, and I try to explain it to him.

I played against a lot of great players, I say. Almost always in playgrounds and schoolyards during the summer when great players were just staying in shape and were looking for a run. Guys like that just wanted to get a thorough workout and were not looking to dominate the competition or embarrass anyone or get into a tong war. They just wanted a good run. But some guys always want to test themselves against other guys, and often when there was a really fine player on the court guys would go at him, and sometimes the great player would just cruise, stone faced, not rising to the bait, but occasionally he would get a little annoyed or weary of the challenge and then he would just change gears and elevate his game and you would get a painfully clear and inarguable lesson in the difference between good and great. A guy like that has gears that you cannot even *imagine*. I mean, I had three gears—lazy, engaged, and intense—and the concept of being able to shift smoothly and easily and without apparent effort into higher gears was incomprehensible to me.

And the first guy who did that while I was playing against him was Kevin Green. He was a very good ballplayer, high-school star, went on to play for the University of Maine, but he didn't get drafted, and he didn't play pro overseas, or play minor league; he was just a good college player, although *just* is an unfair word there; good college players are *very* good ballplayers, believe me.

This was west of Boston. It was a lovely cold crisp spring day. The court was shadowed by huge oak trees. It was on the edge of a golf course; I remember the steady patter of golf balls being mishit and rattling through and against and around the trees, and the faint sound of cursing out on the course. My friend Bill and I were shooting around. Kevin Green wandered by. He was the kid brother of a friend of mine. We challenged him to a game. He grinned and offered to play us one on two. We grinned and thought that good as he was reputed to be, two alert guys should easily swamp one guy. We started well. The game seemed even. And then Kevin Green ever so lightly, ever so casually, ever so undramatically, shifted gears, and without apparent effort he knifed between us for layups, and spun around us without showmanship or flash, and drilled shots from everywhere, and he wiped us out, and then he shook hands and ran off, and I never forgot that day. You would think that two guys being hammered by one younger guy would be embarrassing, but it wasn't at all. It was strangely refreshing and even moving. If you love basketball, you have to love seeing it played with such an economy of motion, such easy effortless power and quickness and deftness, such efficiency, such disciplined grace. It was something to admire even as we got hammered. In a way I have always thought of that game as a victory. I mean, we got smoked, but it was sort of an honor to be on the court with a guy like that. So: the best player I ever played against? Adrian Dantley, I guess—talk about smooth and efficient and unstoppable. But somehow it's Kevin Green who is the deeper answer for me. I saw something that day I had never seen up close before, and it was a pleasure, a lesson, an epiphany; it was actually, to be honest, a delight.

The Guy in the Wheelchair

One time when I was in college I went to go play basketball at the old wooden student gym on a Saturday morning. There were three guys stretching and shooting around at one basket and one guy in a wheelchair shooting at another basket. That guy in the wheelchair had a friend with him who was, I guess, supposed to rebound, but the guy in the chair was drilling shots from the foul line and the friend didn't have much to do. I wondered if the guy in the chair had range farther than the foul line but didn't think I'd find out.

The three guys and I decided to run two on two full court, but just as we were about to start, the guy in the wheelchair said why don't you split us up and play three on three? So we did. The other team picked the friend, who was a big guy, and we got the guy in the wheelchair. His name was Ben. We talked for a moment about how to play. He said listen, I'll just stay at one end, and you guys play a zone. My buddy can't shoot at all. He's a great guy but he's not a ballplayer. On offense get me the ball and then cut and space and I'll get it to you. If they leave me alone I can hit short shots. Use me as a pick if you want. Nobody knocks over a guy in a wheelchair.

We played hard for the next hour and it turned out the guy in the wheelchair was good; he was a lot better passer than you would think a guy sitting in a chair would be, and he hit easily half his shots, and his friend was indeed awful, though cheerful, and we won two of three. But what stays with me is this awkward sentence: the guy in the wheelchair was an ass. He talked trash, he cursed a lot, he held guys as they tried to cut past him, and he berated me once when I missed the world's easiest layup to win a game. He was a good ballplayer, no question about it, and this would be amazing enough, considering that he was sitting in a chair while we were sprinting and whirling around him, but he was a majorly rude and arrogant jerk. None of the guys on the other team shook his hand after the game, not even his buddy, which tells you something. Nor did we, and we were his teammates.

I went to get water and ended up talking to the guy's buddy. I said good game and he said Ben would be fun to play with if he would just shut his mouth the whole game. Ben's a decent guy off the court but he's a horse's ass on it, pretty much.

I said I knew guys like that and you wanted to admire their intensity but it was a royal pain playing with and against them. You almost wanted to walk them outside and have a little firm chat about not being such an ass on the court. But gyms don't have mafia bosses and who you are is who you are. If you can play then you play, though no one ever chooses you again if they can help it.

People always think Ben's working out some rage or something but he was an ass on the court before the crash, said his buddy. You almost have to admire his consistency.

Was he a good ballplayer before?

Eh. He's a lot better now. Now he only does what he can do. He wasn't like that before.

Right about then he and Ben had to leave and I watched from the window as the buddy pushed Ben down the quad toward their hall. For a while I thought about things like arrogance and patience and rage and tenderness and how horse's asses come in all shapes and sizes and probably can't be explained by even the brightest psychological brilliance. Then we ran a last game two on two full court and I went back to my hall thinking about how whatever we think we know for sure about other people is probably not much, or wrong, or both.

Halftime

The greatest halftime speech I ever heard was a brief terse blunt one from a teammate after our red-faced apoplectic splenetic coach had delivered a stemwinder that touched on character, Jesus, willpower, Moses, long hair, Bob Cousy, bandannas, Thomas Jefferson, fancy leather sneakers, Iwo Jima, the insidious horror of earrings on young men, Agincourt, behind-the-back passes, and the Battle of Tolvajärvi, in 1939, when four thousand Finns defeated twenty thousand Russians in the Winter War, which no one remembers, boys, but we will remember it today, for we are the courageous and heroic Finns, and Saint William the Abbot is the damned Red Army, and they are inarguably and indisputably bigger, but we will use guile and creativity and stubborn courage to defeat them, boys, we will attack them where they are weak, we will attack them where they do not expect an attack, we will refuse to cede ground though every shred of sense and reason dictates that we retreat, but we will *not* retreat, because why, boys? Because are Saint John Vianney, dammit! We are the men of Saint John, and that means something in this tumultuous world, and we will prevail, we will win, we will achieve a memorable victory over the dark forces, *if* you stop throwing those candyass behind-the-back passes, and hammer the boards like I have told you to a thousand times since the first day of practice, and stop admiring your shooting form after you take a ludicrous shot from a ridiculous distance, and take off those damned bandannas, and take that candyass earring out of your ear, and play *some* sort of defense that actually entails staying between your man and the basket, and denying him the ball, and cutting off their damned passing lanes, and boxing out their damned center, who is killing us all by himself, and if any *one* of you forwards wants to step up in the second half and make a *hint* of an effort to help out in the lane, any sort of gesture of support at *all*, why, that would be a pleasure, boys, that would warm this old heart of mine, that would give me something to think about on the damned bench other than the way in which our damned guards are lollygagging around out there admiring their shooting form, and taking shots from the damned Arctic Circle instead of driving to the basket, which I have begged you to do since the beginning of time. That's all I have to say. It's your team, boys, not mine, but if *I* was sitting there where you are, *I'd* be heartily ashamed of myself after such a candy-ass first half, each and every one of you, except our center, who is working his tail off, but you decide for yourselves what sort of men you want to be in this life, boys. I can't decide that for you. You think real hard about that. Be back on the court in two minutes.

And he slammed the wooden door behind him as left. This took a herculean effort, I should note, as the door was made of some ephemeral wood like bamboo or balsa or cork, and even when someone slammed it with all his might it made a soft friendly surprised sound like a soap bubble popping or an infant belching milk.

We sat there silent for a little while, and then our center, who had indeed been working his tail off against the best center in the league, said gently, well, let's go to a zone, and you guys drive and dish, and if someone boxes out the Red Army I will get the boards, OK? We good? Let's go.

And we went.

Laces

I was in a gymnasium recently with a gaggle of very small boys, watching them shoot around wildly and gigglingly before their basketball practice, when I saw a tiny-not-tiny moment that I find, weeks and weeks later, unforgettable. Why is it that the slightest things are the ones we remember best in the end? Why is that? I mean, sure we remember the fraught light on our wedding days, and where we were standing when evil news arrived, and the surge of fright and delight when we got the job, or the baby was born, or the tumor was benign; but you know what I mean when I say that we remember far better the exact perfect way to make sandwiches for each child, one with hardly *any* peanut butter and another with butter *and* peanut butter and third with *only* peanut butter, and the way your grandfather whickered like an asthmatic horse when he was amused, and how Saturday morning light arrived at a different angle than weekday light when you were a kid in bed, and how your brothers slowly waking in their beds sounded very much like bears lumbering blearily awake in the remotest snowiest canyons of the West.

The coach blew his whistle—another sharp sound loaded with meaning and memory and shrill and sprint and sweat and sore—and the boys shambled to center court for what promised to be an inspirational speech from the coach, who looked pregnant with wisdom. But then I saw the tiny-not-tiny moment. A dad was kneeling on the sideline retying his son's shoelaces. The shoelaces were orange. The sneakers were blue. The father was bent over the laces like he was praying. The son was perhaps six years old. He was perhaps four feet high. He was staring at his teammates. They were not looking at him. His hands were on his father's shoulders. Perhaps the father was saying something to his son but I couldn't hear. I was that father. I was that son. All at once I desperately wanted the boy to look down at his father with tenderness and love and reverence. I wanted this with all my heart and soul. Just for an instant I wanted the boy to *see* his father, to get the dimmest vaguest sense of the mystery kneeling at his feet and making sure the laces were tight and double- or even triple-knotted so there were no loose ends. It turns out you cannot tie up all the loose ends as a dad but you sure can try. The dad finished one sneaker and went to work on the other and then the boy glanced down at his father. I was sitting a ways away so I couldn't see the boy's face clearly, and maybe he was impatient or embarrassed or muttering something low in his throat like *Hurry up dad!*, but maybe not, you know? Maybe not. Maybe just for an instant, even though he was only six years old, even though he was in a hurry to get onto the court, even though his dad was taking an agonizingly long time to tie his laces, maybe he looked down at his dad and got a jolt of something that I cannot find the right word for, something that defines and elevates and rivets us, something bigger than us, something the boy, if he was lucky, would someday feel the other way around, too.

The dad finished and looked up and seemed about to say something but the boy flew out onto the court, almost hopping over his dad in his hurry, and the dad stood up slowly. Maybe then he sat down in the bleachers to watch, or maybe he slipped out to run errands until practice was over, but I didn't see, because to my surprise I was so moved that I had to go walk up and down the hallway for a while, looking at photographs of all the boys who had played basketball in this gym over the years, arranged in order all the way back to 1911, which was, as you know, only twenty years after the game was invented, on a winter day, in Massachusetts.

Playing Ball in New Jersey

One time for no particular reason at all my friends and I decided to go play basketball in New Jersey. Part of it was that it was a lazy summer Sunday and we had no summer league game that night, and part of it was that one of us could borrow his brother's Plymouth Barracuda if we did it swiftly and quietly by rolling it down the street before starting the engine, and part of it was the very idea of New Jersey, where none of us had ever been, or thought we ever would go. Why would anyone go to Jersey, unless you were running from the police, or wanted to touch Frank Sinatra's house, or had the sudden urge to open a pumpkin stand?

But once the idea was loose it was irresistible, so we borrowed the Barracuda, and got our hoop stuff, and headed to New Jersey. We had not the slightest idea of where it actually was, nor did we have a map—the only map in the car, it turned out, was of Philadelphia, with mysterious hiero-glyphics on it, and cryptic margin notes probably having to do with drugs or pumpkins—so we just headed into Manhattan, on the theory that lots of people from Jersey *worked* in Manhattan, so there must be a road by which they arrived, right? Once in the city the most innocent-looking of us pilfered a map from a tourist shop, and we flipped a coin between the Holland and Lincoln Tunnels. I remember making an eloquent case, from the back seat, for the Lincoln Tunnel, considering who it was named for, whereas the etymology of the Holland Tunnel was a mystery (it turns out it was named for Clifford Holland, who died of a heart attack at age forty-one from the strain of the work), but the front seat went for the Holland, because it ended in Jersey City, and Jersey City was almost sure to actually be in New Jersey, right?

After what seemed to be seven or eight weeks in the tunnel we emerged in Jersey City and then just drove around looking at people, trying to see if they were any different from people in New York. I am not sure now what we expected to see—people carrying pumpkins, perhaps—but as far as we could tell people were pretty much the same in Jersey as in New York. We stopped at a sports bar and asked the bartender for the best basketball parks and he said, in a blunt accent that sounded like he used to live in Staten Island, what color guys you want to play? We said we didn't care, we just wanted a serious run, and he said you want to lose, go to Pershing, you want to win, go to Five Corners. We took this as a challenge and went to Pershing Park, which was battered and ratty and bedraggled and the court was pitted and the basket had no nets and one rim was too low and the other was too high, but you would not believe the quality of play, and we played all afternoon, winning slightly more than we lost, maybe. One of our guys, the guy who had borrowed his brother's Barracuda, dunked a rebound on the low basket and not one but two of the guys on the other team used foul and vulgar language as a compliment, which in basketball is a very high compliment indeed. Finally at dusk we were exhausted and we drove home drinking cold cans of Rheingold beer and talking about the exquisite timing you need to be able to dunk a rebound cleanly. Not only do you have get high enough above the rim to dunk, but you have to be a good enough judge of angle and carom that you anticipate the bounce. It helps when you know the shooter, said the driver to me. I knew you would miss that shot long, because you were way beyond your range from the corner, and I knew you would put too much leg into it, so . . . He said this just as we emerged from the Lincoln Tunnel onto Thirty-Ninth Street, and I remember all four of us laughing at once just as the tunnel ended and we popped out into the gleam and shout of New York City.

This Unconscious Sureness

Having properly boxed out my own man, and ever so gently held the jersey of my teammate's man, whom my teammate has failed to properly box out, I get the rebound, and, being vaguely aware that the lane is crowded with guys going for the rebound, and that the shot was taken by the other team's point guard, who is now sprawling out of bounds, I figure that if I burst out of the pack with the ball and get a jump on the crowd, there may be only a straggler or two back on defense, and indeed this is the case, as I discover when I get to half court, still at high speed, and take a split second to ponder the situation.

I have flown out of the pack headlong and hurried, with my head down, but now that I can feel open space, I look up and see exactly what I did not even bother to think or hope or dream would happen, because I *knew* it would happen, because I knew my teammates and they knew me, and I *knew* they would have seen me burst out of the crowd under the basket and into the open floor, and the instant they saw that I had the ball and was away free they would have sprinted with all their might not only toward our basket, but unconsciously drifting to either side of where I would be, in the middle of the floor, because they knew, again without conscious thought but from a thousand previous plays like this, that I would take the middle, and they should give me central space in which to make a play, which would entail a pass to a sudden cutter, or a pass to one of them standing alone in the corner, or, most likely, as usual, me hogging the ball and driving right to the basket.

But this time, this time, a lovely subtle thing happens, and I am reminded of it this morning because I have been watching tree swallows swooping and looping crossed paths over the fresh-cut summer grass. This time, this time, I stop suddenly, freezing the defender in front of me, who thinks that I might shoot, in which case he had better be ready to contest the shot; but behind him now there is a little chess match happening so blunt and sudden that we should slow down to appreciate the wit and physics of it: my two teammates, who have been sprinting straight down their sidelines, suddenly cut right at each other; the one defender between them, who has been trying to keep an eye on both, is now forced to commit to one, which he does, but that teammate, now hawked by the rattled defender, continues on right out of the play, as the other teammate, unguarded, gathers the bounce pass I threw the instant I saw them cut toward each other, and lays it in.

Whenever I talk about basketball there's something so deeply true about the game that I don't know how to articulately explain it. It has something to do with the fact that I knew what they would do, and they knew what I would do, and none of us had to signal the others, or gesture, or shout, or even think about what to do, but we just did it, because we had played together for years, and knew each other, and trusted each other, and even now, many years after I last played basketball, when someone asks me what I miss the most about it, I want to say, This is what I miss, this unconscious sureness, this unspoken language, this cheerful trust. I miss many other things about the game, but that is what I miss the most.

The Cricket Lover

One time when I was young my friends and I went to play basketball in Queens, at a park where we had heard there were intense games all day long, seven days a week. We were young and strong, and we thought we were good, and we were at the age and stage where you want to test your good against other goods to see who is best: the ancient male urge behind endless bloody battles and weeping children; but perhaps sport will put war out of business eventually, it being much more fun to play basketball than it is to be shot in the groin and bleed to death screaming for your mother.

Indeed the games there were intense, and the players were very good, and we played for an hour, holding court for four games in a row before a loss. We took a break and then got into another intense game, this time against two guys with shaved heads and two guys with dreadlocks. As we were warming up I asked one of the dreadlocks if they were Rastafarians and he said no but they were Jamaican, both born on the island. He was a good guy and we chatted a while and he told me how they'd come to New York City together when they were little, and learned basketball as a sort of language with which to talk American. On the island we played cricket, he said, but no one plays cricket here. I miss it. My friend misses it more. He still dreams about it. I think you can tell he's a cricket lover from the way he plays basketball. You watch.

I did watch, curious about how cricket, a sport I'd never seen, could influence basketball. The cricket lover was a lean quick slippery guy, one of those ballplayers who gets wherever he wants to smoothly and easily and instantly, and for a while I wondered if this effortless quickness was what his friend meant. Then I began to notice two things: he had snake hands, quicker than the eye could follow, and he was always, always, slightly ahead of the play; no matter where the ball went, he was there first, stealing it, getting a hand on it, tipping it to his teammates. He wasn't much of a scorer, but he was such a pain on defense that we lost.

I chatted with his friend afterward and told him I noticed the snake hands and the eerie anticipation, and his friend said that's the cricket—you have to make catches barehanded in cricket, and you learn a sort of ferocious attention to the speed and angle of the ball. Both as a batter and a fielder you must learn to instantly gauge the probable play, and react accordingly. If only he could shoot or dribble he would be a hell of a basketball player. But luckily he doesn't mind only playing defense, and we love playing with him because we get more shots, and usually we win because he's such a disruptive defender.

No one was waiting to play winners so we played them again and lost again. This time I covered the cricket lover and he covered me; I figured I could cruise on defense and expend all my energy trying to score on the guy. But it was like playing a spider six feet tall; no matter where I went, he was already there, and no matter what I tried, he was constantly ticking and nicking at the ball, and throwing me off, and sabotaging the play. We shook hands afterward and talked about cricket for a while. His eyes lit up when I mentioned it and he talked about his favorite players and the joy of playing on the beach and playing on a real cricket pitch, and how even now when he heard a baseball hit hard he thought for an instant that he was back on the island getting ready to play. I told him I would seek out the game and learn to speak it at least a little, and he said that would be a kind gesture for which he was grateful. Then we all had to leave but even now sometimes when I hear a hard-hit baseball I remember how his face lit up when I said the word *cricket*. It was like I had named the girl he adored more than any other.

Hook

It was my brother Kevin who taught me how to shoot a hook shot. The hook is one of the oddest and most difficult shots in basketball, because you cannot see the ball when you shoot it, unlike all the other shots, except the desperate over-the-shoulder flip you shoot when you are passing through the lane and are (a) in the air with no clear idea where you are going or why, or (b) flitting through a thicket of intent defenders with no angle whatsoever at the basket, or (c) you just went up for a layup and got hammered and now you are still airborne but turned completely around so that you are gazing out toward half court, where your lazy defender is still wondering how in the world you got past him. In any of these situations you might as well just flip a shot over your shoulder as you scuttle past the basket, on general principle, because (d) that will avoid the certain turnover you are about to commit, (e) your burly forwards might very well convert the rebound into an easy bucket, for which you can claim credit or even claim an assist if you are feeling brave, or (f) it might actually drop in, which not only gives you two points you never expected but also gives you the chance to say straight-faced to your teammates that you knew it would go in because you have secretly been practicing this shot, which is a whopping lie.

As I remember, my brother Kevin had come to one of the first organized league games I played, and noticed that I had neither hide nor hair of a hook, even though I was spending a good deal of time in the lane, and he set out to teach me the hook at the basket attached to our garage. First he walked me through the odd motion of it—you turn ninety degrees *away* from the basket, and toss the shot up from behind your head with a sweeping motion of your arm. This seemed insane to me and I said so and he made me do it another fifty times. Then he made me try it left-handed but concluded quickly that asking me to do anything left-handed was a fool's game. Back we went to the right hand. He taught me to extend my left arm for stability and to fend off the defender, and take the proper two steps before hoisting up the shot. He taught me to gauge the arc of a shot that is essentially taken blind, which is a hard thing to do. He delivered a long and articulate sermon about how the shot is really all about feel and repetition and rhythm, and how you will never hit it consistently unless you relax and just flip it up there easily, "like," he said, in a line that still makes me laugh, "you are tossing a toaster up to someone on the next floor of the apartment building"—a line that makes you wonder just how he knew that.

All that week he made me take fifty hooks a day after school, even though it was growing bitterly cold, and on Saturday he took me to my game against, as I recall, Saint Mary Star of the Sea from Far Rockaway. Before the game he said that he expected me to take at least one hook during the game, and if I shot it right we would stop for ice cream on the way home. You don't even have to hit it, he said. You just have to shoot it right.

Early in the second half I got the ball in the lane with a gawky skinny defender draped all over me, and I took the proper two steps and stuck my arm out and jabbed the guy sharply in the throat, and I hoisted up the shot, and the defender made a strangled glorking sound like he was going to barf, and the shot rolled out, but one of our forwards collected it and scored, and after the game Kevin was so tickled at how I had shot the thing right, and how my elbow had nailed the guy right on the Adam's apple, that we stopped for ice cream. Technically you nailed him right between the thyroid cartilage and the cricoid cartilage, he said, the former of which protects the larynx, but anyway you shot that ball perfectly, and that's what counts. You play the game right and good things will happen. Didn't you think that guy was going to barf? I sure did.

A Brief Note on Shorts

Yes, there *were* guys who played basketball while wearing pants—jeans or sweats or the occasional khakis, and once, horrifyingly, glowing yellow capri pants, although in that case no one laughed because the guy sporting them had muscles on his muscles, plus this was in Chicago where anything was possible, and plus he wasn't half-bad, perhaps because you couldn't see well when he was near you, his pants were that bright. I mean, who would seek out and actually purchase glowing yellow capri pants? Not to mention they were loose and baggy so that it sure looked like he was wearing culottes. But again no one saw fit to remark on this phenomenon, or say the word *culottes*, fine a word as it is, *Vive la France*, and he left after one game, anyway.

But almost every other guy I ever played with or against wore shorts, and you would not believe the variety of shapes and colors and fabrics of those shorts. Some guys wore what clearly were their uniform shorts from leagues. Lots of guys wore shorts that they had stolen from athletic entities, be they schools, colleges, athletic clubs, branches of the armed forces, churches, temples, surf shops, and etc. beyond measure. Lots of guys especially in cities wore denim shorts that clearly had once been the upper third of blue jeans. Twice that I remember, a guy wore boxer shorts. Once I played against a guy who wore a brief-style bathing suit, and I vividly remember that no one wanted to cover him, and we ended up flipping a coin for the dubious privilege, and the guy who had to cover him was useless defensively, but we understood. But mostly it was shorts, and one reason that I am happy I stopped playing when I was thirty, many years ago, is that I never had to endure guys wearing their shorts low and saggy and falling off, or play against a guy wearing the billowing mainsails that seem fashionable today, for reasons that elude me, because wearing shorts that force you to tack sharply to the starboard in a stiff breeze does not seem like fun to me, nor does it seem to be assistive in any way in the conduct of the beautiful game.

In Chicago once I played against a guy who was wearing a red towel, and I remember that he never once had to adjust or tighten or rewrap it, which is mysterious: did he have it pinned, or sewn tight, or was it glued to his skin, or maybe was it even *sewn to his skin*, could that be? It doesn't seem possible, but, again, this was Chicago, so.

The worst thing about the shorts that you played against and sometimes with was that they had never been washed since the dawn of time, and you could tell this easily, in fact you could tell from half a mile away if the wind was right, but then again it's not like you washed *your* shorts after every game. My own rule was once a week, which sounds reasonable except for the fact that I played two hours a day every day, and only had one pair of shorts, so that when the week began I was clean and tall and virtuous, and by Saturday I seemed to have much more room to maneuver on the court, and children and dogs fled from me when I ran home after playing ball. One time I stopped on my way home to admire a towering sunflower, which then crumpled and died before my eyes. This sounds farfetched, I am sure, but that also happened in Chicago, so.

A Small-Not-Small Moment

Here's a basketball story. Maybe it's a small story but I never forgot it and I bet you won't forget it, either. It's not very dramatic. It was in high school. Varsity basketball tryouts. The tryouts were reluctantly open to the entire student body even though the entire student body knew that the team was set in stone, the coach had his twelve guys, he had his starters picked out, he knew his rotation, he knew which sophomore would be the luckless twelfth guy on the varsity, he knew which juniors would slowly be given more minutes over the course of the season to groom them for next year's starting slots; he knew which senior would be the eleventh guy and never play a minute except in blowouts, starting only the very last game of his career, in a gesture that the coach thought magnanimous but the senior, I happened to know, thought, in the end, dismissive and careless and thoughtless.

Tryouts were three days long, with cuts at the end of each session. Sessions were two hours long with the first hour being drills and the second hour being scrimmages. Scrimmages started out evenhanded and then the varsity starters came in and hammered the surviving candidates. The system was fair and cold; if a candidate could not hold his own and show some spark against the starters, why should he be considered for the team? And one by one the candidates found their names posted on the window of the gym an hour after the tryout session; eight names the first day, five the second day.

But fourteen boys had shown up for the open tryouts, which meant one was left for the third day. This was a boy named Chris. He was a long lean almost gaunt guy with long hair that flopped and whirled when he played.

He hardly ever said a word but grinned a lot on the court even when the starters tried to hammer him. It seemed to me, though, that they could never quite get a solid shot in on Chris—he was slippery and shadowy and somehow managed to get where he wanted to be without undue effort and exertion, and he had the most efficient effective outside shot I had ever seen; maybe I am wrong, but it sure seemed like every time he got the slightest open look he drilled the shot, and he had extraordinary range.

That third session drew a crowd—not only the boys who had been cut over the last two days, who had come to like Chris and root for him, but also a lot of other students who either knew Chris and liked him, or had heard the story about how he was the last man standing, the last of us, our avatar, our agent trying to scale the granite cliff of the coach and his program, which had been his construct and his bailiwick and his fiefdom for years. There were even a few teachers and staffers there to watch the last session—interested in the drama, perhaps, or maybe people who didn't much like the coach, and hoped for a shiver in the usual script.

Chris held his own through the drill hour, never first but never last in sprints and defensive drills and such; and he was one of the two or three best players in the opening scrimmages, with and against varsity substitutes and junior varsity starters. Then the coach set his starters against Chris and four of the varsity substitutes for a final scrimmage.

By this time I bet there were a hundred people in the gym, which doesn't sound like much, except that the bleachers were all folded up and everyone was standing around the court and behind the baskets. There was a curious silence; I remember that particularly because high school kids are never silent in numbers, and it was a remarkable absence of sound—almost a loud silence.

The varsity that year was very good—three of the starters went on to play college ball, and one even went on to play pro overseas, from what I heard— and they got out to a good lead against Chris and the subs. But then the subs roared back and took the lead. I think now that their elevated play was about saying something to the coach that they could never say in words, but there's no question it also had to do with Chris, who was hitting his shots but even better passing deftly and creatively to guys who seemed much more alert to cuts than they usually were.

The starters geared up, though, and won the scrimmage by a couple of buckets, and the gym emptied slowly, but then there was a small-not-small moment. I was one of the last students out of the gym, and I had turned to see who would hit the last shot—it's an old basketball superstition that you cannot leave a court without someone hitting a last shot, you want to leave the basket with a memory of the ball, something like that—and I noticed Chris hitting one long shot after another. One of the substitutes was snapping the ball back to him as it dropped through the hoop, and Chris hit five in a row, ten, twenty, thirty, and then he stepped back behind the top of the key and hit five straight, before walking off the court and shaking hands with the substitute, and turning and staring at the coach.

Of course Chris's name was on the cut list on the window an hour later. Of course it was. It sat there all alone on the sheet of paper and I bet that sheet of paper stayed in the window for three days. I realized later that Chris knew he would be cut, that probably everyone in the gym knew that he would be cut, and that's why he had passed so generously during the scrimmage, and why he had made a statement to the coach afterwards.

A small story; one teenage kid many years ago, deliberately playing the right way during a scrimmage even though he knew that the only way he would force the issue was to dominate, to be melodramatic, to play the wrong way; and then all those shots, one after another, each one dropping exactly through the hoop from long distances, and then a long look to say something he couldn't say in words. He didn't glare at the coach; he didn't curse or say anything challenging or rude; he just stared at him for a long minute—a wonderfully eloquent stare, I thought then, and still think now.

The Black Hole

Everyone who ever played on a basketball team knows what I mean when I say the words *black hole*. A black hole is a region of the basketball court occupied by a gravitational force from which no ball returns once the ball has entered the reach of the black hole. A black hole can be of any size or mass, although in my experience black holes were usually forwards or centers who had sweeping reaches so that any ball thrown within half a mile of them was drawn into their possession even if the ball in question had been thrown to another guy standing within the same half mile.

Sometimes there were black holes who would no-kidding leap to steal passes clearly and inarguably and obviously intended for a teammate. I played with a center once who had this trait, and while it could be enormously frustrating on offense, it was occasionally useful on defense, because while he was not at all interested in defense, and actively and vehemently disliked playing defense, and strenuously objected to defense apparently for religious reasons, and was raging impatient *while* his teammates played defense, and was the kind of guy who would always leak out on breaks hoping that someone else would cover his man so he might get a free basket at the other end, still, once a game or so, while not playing any kind of defense that we could see, he would suddenly leap and steal a pass, and instantly take off with the ball to try to score, whether or not any of us were open ahead of him, or he was being covered, or any of the usual reasons players share the ball with other players, which was not a language he spoke.

Our theory about these interesting moments when he suddenly appeared to be playing a hint or shred or flicker of defense was that he couldn't help himself, being so attuned to the ball passing through his region of gravitational force that the arrival of the ball over his event horizon set off an inevitable reaction that led to him snatching the ball, followed by the irrepressible urge to score, followed sometimes by a hilarious turnover, although to give the man his due he *did* often score when in that situation, usually by pulling up for a long jump shot for no discernable reason other than he loved to shoot every single blessed time he got the ball, which is why we called him the black hole.

On the other hand he was a terrific offensive rebounder, although each and every one of his offensive rebounds immediately turned into another shot attempt for him alone; but still, offensive rebounders are rare and lovely beings, and should be savored when they appear, in the same way that we appreciate comets and asteroids and meteors. A hardworking offensive rebounder, even one who retrieves the ball in burly traffic with the sole intent of padding his own numbers, is an evident and comprehensible phenomenon, whereas a black hole, while theoretically not uncommon, remains an abiding mystery. The inner workings of the black hole, and why exactly he exhibits such a ferocious gravitational force, are a fascinating puzzle, like many other aspects of basketball, for example why our center's right arm did not fall off after taking thirty shots in forty minutes, and why the tallest forward we ever played with did not snare a single rebound that we remember in the two complete seasons we played with him in a tough league where God knows we could have used a few boards from a starting *forward* for heaven's sake but who is bitter? Not me. Certainly not me.

Mongo

Speaking of low moments, I am reminded of a basketball game in Boston, in a tough league in which a lot of guys had played college ball. I had played poorly the whole game, and just been called for a fourth foul after being creamed by a large burly opponent nicknamed Mongo, and something snapped in my fervid brainpan, yet again, as happened fairly regularly on the basketball court, I think because I loved the game so much and got immensely frustrated when I did not play well, and I bided my time, and then, when Mongo's attention was elsewhere, I crashed into him as hard as I could, elbows up. He was staggered, but then he recovered, and he swung at me, and he was ejected, and I had fouled out, so we both stalked angrily to our benches.

Usually right about here is where contretemps on basketball courts end, as benches are good places to simmer and stew and calm down eventually and begin to regret that you were such a horse's ass, but not this time, not with me, for I took the long way around to our bench, making sure to pass slowly in front of the other team's bench, taunting the entire other team and saving particularly lewd and vulgar insults for Mongo, who turned as purple as the regal color of imperial robes, before he was restrained by his teammates, and I plopped down on our bench next to my friend Pete.

What, said Pete quietly, is the matter with you? Why do you do this? What is wrong with you? You do this all the time. Why would you bait a guy named Mongo? Do you not think the name Mongo indicates something of the nature of the man? A guy named Mongo is the kind of guy who waits outside after the game and tries to take your teeth out with his head. Why do you lose your mind? You are *not* actually a muscular guy and yet you bait the other team and curse at the refs and lose your mind and foul out and where is any of this fun and helpful? What exactly is your problem? You are a good ballplayer when you keep cool and just play but you *don't* keep cool, you lose your mind, and who suffers for it? *We* suffer for it. *You* don't suffer. I am going to check back in to the game and the first thing that will happen is that some clown will hammer me as punishment for you. How is this fun for me? The other team will play twice as hard now. You just couldn't let it go. You had to get your revenge. You didn't get it that the best revenge is playing well and winning the game. Now you are out of the game and the other team is pissed and Mongo will probably wait outside for you after the game. We are going to have to walk out with you to make sure no one beats you up. I hate fistfights. Fistfights are stupid. This is not the school-yard. What's the matter with you? You had a happy childhood, you have a job, we went to college, girls don't hate you, why do you act this way? What are you trying to prove? Why in heaven's name would you smash a guy named *Mongo*? Why do you pick out the biggest meanest guy and start up with him? Are you nuts? I have to go back in the game now. Thanks for the next four fouls I am going to absorb because of you. You need to get a grip. And don't tell me you get frustrated because you love the game so much. If you loved the game enough you would treat it with respect, instead of being such a horse's ass. Think about *that* for a while. Sub!

I did think about that for a while, and in a sense I have been thinking about it ever since, and today, while I remember that as a particularly low moment among many, I also remember it as the start of not having such low moments again, that I remember. And now I realize that while I have always been grateful to Pete, who has remained one of my dearest friends, I should also probably be grateful to Mongo, too, wherever he is; meeting him did start me on the road of not being such a horse's ass, for which I am happy, and for which, all these years later, I say thanks.

The Flowing Chess of the Game

Some years ago I was visiting a monastery in Sydney, Australia. The monastery crowned a gentle hill over the vast and sprawling harbor. There were gum trees and parrots and fruit bats and arboreal marsupials called brushtail possums, which were officially nocturnal and shy but did not prove to be either of those things at the monastery, where they wandered into the kitchen in the morning and quietly ate from a bowl filled with eggs every morning for them.

The monastery abutted a school and the burble of voices from the children rose and fell during the day at set times marked by bells. I got into the habit of walking through the fields set aside for cricket and rugby and watching the matches with the eager pleasure of a man who had never seen either sport up close and was riveted by the geometry and vocabulary and hurly-burly of pursuits he did not know but was interested to try to understand without formal instruction. The rugby I could understand fairly easily, it being essentially militaristic and the clear ancestor of American football. The cricket, while also clearly the ancestor of American baseball, was another matter altogether, with one pitcher but two batters, and fielders scattered every which way, and batters running bases with their bats, and the pitcher doing his or her utmost to hit not the catcher's mitt but a triad of spindly sticks behind the batter. All this as green and red parrots rocketed past, and the alluring spice of eucalyptus lofted through the air, as did the ancient song of bells, and the chatter and rattle of a language all around me in which I knew the words but not the music; an odd and entertaining and occasionally deeply unnerving feeling, like being in a familiar boat in a strange sea.

One day in my rambles I found the school's tiny basketball court, in a copse of sassafras and bottlebrush trees. There were four boys playing on it, and I stopped to watch, as I love basketball above all other games, love its grace and humor and creativity and generosity and simplicity, a game with no pads or helmets or specialized equipment, a game you can play alone for hours, a game that anyone anywhere can grasp and play in moments, a game that can be played beautifully by anyone of any size, a game that does not reward violence, a game that does reward selflessness and inventiveness and speed and liquidity.

I watched for twenty minutes, admiring the quality of the athletes but not the quality of their play; it seemed to me that the boys, perhaps age seventeen, were quick and strong and supple, but they were not versed in the angles and shiftiness of the game; I remember wondering if they were new to it, and that very night a monk in the kitchen confirmed exactly that, that basketball was a poor sister to rugby and cricket and Australian football at the school, and probably in Australia at large, the vast country savoring its old imperial sports and its one native sport, Australian football having been invented there as a marriage of aboriginal and settler games, as far as he could tell, though there were many theories about that.

The next afternoon I went down to the basketball court again and found the same four boys, but this time they hailed me, and we got to talking about the game, and they asked me to show them some of the *patterns*, as one boy said. I confessed that as a player myself I had been terrible at running plays, and only in my older age had my appreciation for the flowing chess of the game deepened wonderfully; but then with pleasure I walked them through common plays like a backdoor cut, and a double pick, and showed them how one player can set a screen for another player to shoot behind, and how two players can spring a trap on a ballhandler, and how one player can box out his man so that his teammate has a clear path to a rebound, and a few other basic things like that; and then they happily applied my teaching for a while in scrimmage, before the bell rang and they sprinted back up the hill to the school.

In this life I have spent about thirty days in Australia, some seven hundred hours, I suppose, and I relished almost all of those hours, and think of them often—the sharp angle of a different sun, the new stars at night, the procession of dinosauric bats overhead at night, the pelting of parrots through the trees, the rough cheerful wit and kindness of the citizenry, the paw prints of new animals in the moist soil at dawn, the extraordinary sight of a brushtail possum silently eating an egg in one corner as an elderly monk sipped his coffee and read the morning newspaper in the other; but as long as I live, I think, I hope, I will also remember, with a deep and abiding pleasure, the hour that I was, for once, a teacher of a lovely and gracious subject. I hope that at least one of those boys remembered what I taught him, and used the lessons later in his play, and himself occasionally now vaguely remembers the older American man who paused one day, under the sassafras and bottlebrush trees, and taught him new words in a language he was just beginning to speak.

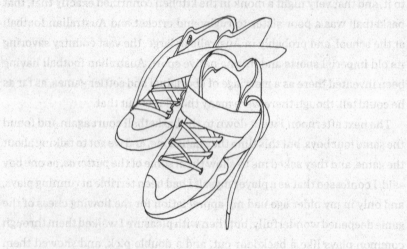

The Fast Break

You would *think* that if a guy has the ball on a fast break, and has two team-mates sprinting along either wing, and his big lunk of a center lumbering along dutifully behind him to clean up rebounds if necessary, and the last teammate hanging back just in case the play goes to hell and someone better be back at free safety to cut off a counterstrike, that he, the guy with the ball, who is not necessarily me although alright, fine, it's me, would quickly scan the possible plays he could make, and then, having a great deal of experience on breaks, make the best of his options, and lead one of the cutters with a sharp pass in just the right spot so he, the cutter, could catch it in stride and lay it in, or catch up to a floating pass and lay it in, or he, the guy with the ball, could get cute and drive right to the hole but at the last possible instant flip it up over his shoulder for the trundling lunk to catch and dunk, or more likely catch and drop out of bounds because he, the lunk, has hands of stone and couldn't catch a cold if you tucked it into his hand like a sparrow, but who is bitter about the thousand passes that lunk has dropped over the years? Certainly not me.

And you would think that even if he, the guy with the ball, does not make a sharp pass to one of his cutters, or leave the ball hanging behind him for the lunk to punt, that he might drive to the hole and score, or drive and stop and hit that little easy parabolic teardrop shot, or even drive and fake the teardrop and zip it to one the cutters who are now camped in either corner, but you would *not* think that he, the guy with the ball, would do the following: drive to the hole, stop suddenly, fake the teardrop with a vast showy fake that would have made a theater director moan with pleasure, evade his lumbering center who thunders past with a look of total confusion on his face, and then ignore not one but *both* of the former cutters who are now toasting marshmallows and reading Proust in lawn chairs their corners, and, then, just as all five defenders converge with bad intent, *whip the ball through them all the way back out to half court,* where the last teammate catches it in stride, takes two steps, and launches a thirty-footer, which has no business going in but amazingly does, and the shooter, who didn't expect it to drop quite so cleanly either, blows gun smoke from his forefinger, which sets the rest of us to laughing helplessly, which deeply annoys our coach, and further puzzles our poor center, who is still not sure what happened, and will have to have it all drawn up slowly for him later, with colored pencils marking each guy's path and the path of the ball, and a quiz on Friday.

You would not think that this exact play could happen in any known universe, because there were so many other more sensible plays available before this play, and this is the theme of the coach's grim dyspeptic monologue after the game, and we listen respectfully to the coach, because he is a decent soul, if a little stern and linear about basketball, and then when he leaves, closing the door behind him slightly harder than usual to show that he *really* means what he said, we start to laugh again, because our center, who is a lovely guy but not the brightest bulb ever, is still poring over the colored lines, wondering how in heaven's name he did not get the ball, which ended up back near half court, which, on a fast break, doesn't make sense, which is why it was so fun, and why I remember it even today, years later, but, as you see, not.

A Court in West Boston

A son asks me when I played the best basketball of my life, and I say, instantly, without hesitation, *The summer before I turned 28 ...*

And back floods every Saturday morning solo workout with maniacal drills in order to finally develop even a semblance of a left-handed hook, and Sunday afternoon doubleheaders with six guys running full court for two hours and then collapsing in the grass laughing and moaning for beer, and every other evening's headlong run on a beautiful court in west Boston, under elm and oak and maple trees, against guys who were not only my friends but terrific ballplayers, and they were in superb shape then, too, and loose and limber and furiously competitive, and we did not yet have wives and children and serious jobs in which you don't mind staying late because you love the work and it isn't work, so we would assemble casually at dusk, one guy having called two guys who called three others, and there might be a guy or two there we didn't know and we would wrap them into the game, swapping them after a while if one was markedly better than the other;

Or one of our guys might have brought a cousin or a college friend or a friend from work, and almost always those stray guys were better than they appeared to be, perhaps because they had no ego in the game and were there as obvious appendices, so they rebounded hard and played defense and didn't yap and were decent teammates who hustled after balls and didn't call for shots and didn't hack in desperation and often didn't even call fouls even when they were most egregiously and incontrovertibly and inarguably fouled;

And the quality of play was such that sometimes passersby would stop and watch for a while, old folks out for their evening constitutional, or folks walking their dogs, or kids riding their bikes, and occasionally even the local cops, who would pull their cruiser into the pool of dark under the biggest elm and watch us for a while, perhaps remembering when they were young guys in Boston playing ball under the lights and the thick dense salty evening air stuffed with moths and nighthawks and the squeak of sneakers and the cadence of the ball and the muffled code of the players commenting on picks and screens and silly shots and the score and whose turn it is to buy a round at the pub;

And every one of us regulars knew every other one of the regulars and the intricacies and idiosyncrasies of their games and the fitful wrinkles of their habits and characters, and every one of us had seen every conceivable fake and dodge and trick and deke in the other guys' toolboxes, so the games got better and better as the summer went on because each guy had to up his game or else, so you had to invent new moves, and new fakes, and actually play defense, and hustle after balls, and box out, and rebound your shot, because if you did not do these things you would get smoked by your friends, who had no mercy or pity whatsoever on the court, and would have happily and cheerfully and with a deep and abiding pleasure held you scoreless if possible, and scored a hundred baskets on you if possible, because that mercilessness and pitilessness was part and parcel of the joy of the game, that the game was intense and ferocious and muscular and played as hard as you could possibly play, harder than guys had ever played in the various uniforms of various schools, because this was not a game against some other school, some team of faceless guys from another town; this was a game against your boys, your friends, your teammates, your tribe, your other brothers; and young men do nothing quite so ferociously and intently and happily as try, with all their might, with every iota of their strength and effort, with the deepest of joys in their hearts, to defeat their brothers;

And even now, all these years later, when I am no longer loose and limber and supple and muscular and relentless and a youth in the fullness of his minor physical gifts, I feel a jolt of the pleasure of that summer again, just by trying to put it into words. I do not think that writers admit enough that much of what they are trying to do is drape words upon that for which we have no good words, finally; like that summer, that court, those friends, those mammoth elms, the little boy who has hooked his fingers into the metal fence around the court and is watching us with both awe and anticipation; for very soon, in the measure of things, he will be me.

In My Defense

I grasped the *concept* of playing defense on a basketball court from the very start of my motley career; I understood the straightforward principles, I admired the simplicity of the basic premise, that you should stay near your man at all times, ideally between him and the basket, while remaining alert and aware of the ball's movement, and of the ever-present possibility of picks being set behind and around you; I even quickly apprehended the intricacies of shifting zone defenses, the swift calculus of the one-two-two, the box-and-one, the triangle-and-two, the half-court trap, the full-court press; all this I understood, and even enjoyed in theory, much as I loved chess and its endless thrust and counterthrust and ever-shifting patterns; it was lovely to think about how one team might defend itself with a single great shooter, or how you could neutralize another team's greater height, or how you could pack the lane and force a poor-shooting team to try their luck from the arctic regions. The problem for me, though, was that actually *playing* defense was deeply and unendurably boring, and I could never last more than a few seconds before trying to enliven matters by stealing the ball, or abandoning my man to crash a pick, or abandoning my man to sag down on a big guy who was foolishly bringing the ball down below his waist, where us munchkins could swipe at it. Why big guys always wanted to dribble is a mystery to me, but they did, and still do, the poor lumbering mastodons.

I think every coach I ever had sat me down at one point and gave me a speech that went something like this: Son, you are a decent athlete, and you are not a complete idiot, and you appear to understand the basic principle of the two defenses we play—we do not play fifty defenses, we only play two, and they are fairly straightforward in their basic premises—which is to say that a man-to-man means that you *stay with your man*, and a zone means that you *stay in your assigned region of the court*, yet you do not stay with your man, but range about free as a bird, defending no one in particular and going for steals and blocks even though I have asked you one thousand times not to do that, and when we switch to zone you do not stay in your region, but gambol about loose and free, letting your man sit in his rocking chair and drill short uncontested shots all game long, which is giving me gray hair and ulcers, and can you explain why you are so uninterested in any hint or iota of defense? Not to mention that you often do not seem to get the signal from our point guard that we are switching from one defense to another. It is a fairly simple signal, don't you think, a closed fist? Yet you seem to cheerfully set up in whatever defense you think we are in, and then abandon even the appearance of playing that defense, and set about your headlong free-form voyages. Could you possibly explain to me what, if anything, you are thinking about any of this? Son?

But it was hard for me to articulate my feelings about defense, which were complex. First, it was deadly boring to dog just one opponent for long minutes at a time, when there were so very many to swipe at and collide with and exchange vulgar pleasantries with; why defend only one man thoroughly, when you could swipe ineffectually at all five? Second, the first rule of orthodox defense was to stare intently at your man's chest, avoiding looking him in his shifty eyes, ignoring his feints and fakes, all the while doing your utmost to legally interrupt his progress, but all of this sensible stuff, in my view, ignored the thrilling fact that the ball was *right there to be taken*, as alluring a gleaming object as you could imagine, and who would not make a concerted effort to steal such a valuable thing, if you could? Third, what could possibly be cooler than blocking a shot, anyone's shot, so that if a guy ten feet away was lining up a shot, why should I not take a stab at it, whether or not the shooter then instantly delivered the ball to my man for an easy layup, which happened one million times, causing our coach to make that strangled sound in his throat like he was having trouble swallowing a badger?

Fourth, it seemed to me that coaches and point guards put an unseemly emphasis on stopping the other team from scoring, when a much more attractive and entertaining approach was to simply *outscore* the other team. In my view, if I gave up twenty points to the guy I was supposed to be covering on defense, but scored more than twenty myself, I was up on the deal, and I think I am in an unassailable position here, for if we all outscored our guys, we would have more points, and we would win the game, and the coach would not make that strangled sound in his throat as if he had just eaten a kitten-and-mayonnaise sandwich, a sound I knew all too well.

There are many adjectives you could use to describe me as a defender, ranging from lazy to terrible to ridiculous to hilarious to abject to irresponsible to hapless to ludicrous to lunatic, and I am the first to acknowledge that all those adjectives are uncomfortably accurate, but I still maintain that no one ever had more sheer fun playing defense than I did, swiping constantly for steals and constantly earning fouls (you are allowed five, so why not use your entire allowance?), trying to block any shot within the metro area, calling to my teammates to cover my man for me when I lost track of his whereabouts, and other pleasurable things like that. It still makes me smile to remember the way I would cheerfully wave at my teammates and call their attention to my man, as he sailed unobstructed to the basket, and they would gesture back at me animatedly, in those subtle but eloquent signals that ballplayers use when words fail them, and the coach would make that strangled sound in his throat, as if he had just eaten a particularly large fried chipmunk, when he thought he had ordered the smaller snack-sized one, with chips and pickles on the side.

The Seven-Foot Guy

The tallest guy I ever played against was a seven-foot guy who had been in a professional basketball training camp. This was in summer league in Boston. Games were at night on a beautiful court under elm trees. The court was brilliantly lit, but everything outside the glowing box of the court was pitch-dark, so that guys who walked onto the court just *appeared* magically, as if they had been invented on the spot, or sent from another dimension. Sometimes it seemed to me that you could instantly identify a guy's position by the manner in which he entered the bright stage of the court: guards would be dribbling lazily, forwards would be adjusting their elbow pads and billy clubs and brass knuckles, and centers would be trying unsuccessfully to remember their names and the day of the week.

Usually we would pay scant attention as the other team trickled onto their end of the court, but in this case we had heard that they featured a seven-foot guy who'd had a tryout with the Cleveland Cavaliers, so when he popped into the light, looking like he was twenty feet tall, we were impressed; he was indeed one long dude, he looked like he might remember his name, and he immediately casually dunked and stared down at us. We were a confident group, and we had a good center of our own, but our man was easily seven inches shorter than their man, although our man had been to Cornell University and usually knew the day of the week.

One thing I loved about our team then is that we never had the slightest strategy: we had no plays, we never scouted or even really deigned to acknowledge the opposition; we just went out and played as hard and fast as we could, figuring that in general our best was better than the opposition's best, which often turned out to be true. And to my enduring pleasure we began that game against the seven-foot guy without a word about the seven-foot guy.

The seven-foot guy, I report with a smile, turned out to be the slowest guy in the history of basketball, lumbering so ploddingly up and down the court that he was constantly behind the play, whether on offense or defense; our center noticed this immediately and turned the rest of the game into a track meet. But two other things happened that evening that still give me pleasure, all these years later. The first was the way our deft and devious point guard attacked the seven-foot guy with glee and brio and surgical skill. He drove right at him, which reduced the guy's wingspan; he turned him that way and that when he got him out in the open court, one time spinning him around so quickly that the big guy fell down; and he forced the guy to foul him twice, earning four free points at the line. It was a clinic on how a small player can outplay a big player using speed and guile and changes of direction, and luring the bigger player out and away from the lane; that was the first time I realized that a player's height is proportionately reduced by his distance from the basket, and that a big guy out in the open is easy meat.

The second thing was the way that our power forward, a burly chesty muscular guy only an inch or two over six feet tall, took on the herculean task of covering the seven-foot guy on defense. Our center, while a gifted scorer, was a terrible defender, uninterested at the best of times and particularly uninterested that night. But our power forward loved the bang and brawl of rebounding, loved the scrum and grapple of the lane, and loved the chance to frustrate a much bigger and heavier guy. I don't think I ever saw a guy work as hard on a basketball court as our forward did that night. I cannot remember that he scored much, or even hauled down his usual dozen rebounds, for he had set himself to be an immovable barrier and annoyance and roadblock to the seven-foot guy, and he was all of those things in spades.

I remember once sliding through the lane trying to keep track of my own guy, for once, and seeing the ferocious look on our forward's face as he strained to keep the big guy away from the basket. I would have stopped to shake our forward's hand and express my admiration for a really remarkable night's work, but he seemed busy, and not in the mood for pleasantries, and I was rather enjoying the novel experience of playing defense, so I kept going, holding on to the shirt of the guy I was defending, to be sure of his direction. A little later the game ended, and we shook hands with the other guys, and guys vanished back into the darkness magically, as if they'd only existed while on the court.

Shooting

A Note

Jump shot, set shot, hook shot, scoop shot, layup, finger roll, and the alluring bizarre teardrop shot, in which you launch a shot far higher than normal, so as to evade the grasping fingertips of a shot blocker in the lane,
and the ball soars five or eight or ten feet above the rim, a sight you very
rarely see on a basketball court unless a terrible foul shooter is once again
throwing the ball up any old way and making the rest of the players on the
floor weep with laughter, and your shot, the teardrop shot, finally plum-
mets back toward the basket, and, if you have calculated it correctly, drops
cleanly through the hoop, but if you have not calculated it right it bangs off
the rim with a mortifying clang, and soars away in one of those embarrassing rebounds that shouts your inaccuracy, such as when you pull up for a
jumper from the foul line and the shot misses so badly that the rebound
sails back over the backboard and even your teammates try not to laugh as
they retreat back on defense.

And then there are the many permutations of each shot—the drifting
jump shot, attempted while you are floating in one direction or another;
the leaner, which you shoot after your defender has bit on your pump fake
and he flails past and you lean in toward the basket and get the jumper off
right quick before anyone else arrives to argue the matter; the fall-away,
in which you do not for once rise straight up to shoot but actually jump
backward away from your defender while hoisting up a shot only Jesus or
Hakeem Olajuwon could block; the stop-and-pop, in which you are dribbling casually and are seemingly casting about to see the lay of the land and
what the play might be and where your teammates are when suddenly you

just arise from the gleaming hardwood and launch a jump shot that, if it drops, makes you look like a cool calm assassin of a shooter, but if it misses causes your coach to make that strangled sound in his throat like a heron trying to swallow a trout she should have halved but didn't.

And of course each shot can be taken with either hand, which in almost all players makes a tremendous difference in accuracy, so that a player who hits half his jumpers taken with his right hand will hit one of a hundred taken with his left hand, and consider himself lucky to have hit the one; even the best players can barely shoot layups with their off-hand, although curiously hook shots, probably because they are launched without looking at the ball, and entail a looping motion of the arm that you can practice endlessly in business meetings and at church picnics and on trams, lend themselves better to being taken with either hand; every player has, at one time or another, launched a ridiculous hook with the wrong hand, having no other options as the clock ticked down, and watched with astonishment as it dropped through the hoop, and then missed the next fifty of those shots, after mistakenly concluding that he was good at it, which he was not.

And then the dozen or so ways that you can shoot a foul shot, from the ancient but very effective underhand style that no one ever uses because it looks so geeky, to the hilarious ways by which centers bazooka their foul shots, endangering small children and dogs in the stands with their ricocheting rebounds, and occasionally cracking a backboard with the force of a shot that should ideally be launched ever so gently in exactly the same way every time, which is why foul shooters adopt peculiar mannerisms, such as exactly seven dribbles before shooting, or spinning the ball in the exact same way every time, or standing off to one side or another of the foul line, or drying the hands on the shirt the shoes the headband the referee, and ad infinitum; basketball players are among the most superstitious people on Earth, and what works for a player once will be attempted again and again until he finds something else that works for him, which he then adopts until, well, you get the picture.

Then there are such things as the shooter's credo (If you are cold, shoot until you get hot, and if you are hot, keep shooting until you go cold), and the coaches' shooting credo, which is that you should score in close early to get used to the ball going through the basket, and then and only then launch longer shots, and the bench players' shooting credo (Shoot every time you get the ball, to show that you should be a starter), and the star's shooting credo (I should take all the shots, except when I parcel out a shot or two for everyone else because I am generous and magnanimous and handsome), and the lock-down defender's shooting credo (No one on either team should ever shoot, and the final score should be zero-zero, with the game decided by penalty kicks), and many other shooting theories and conspiracies like these, more than even I can remember, and I try to remember everything, because I think we get this one lovely wild life, and should enjoy and savor and relish every moment of it, especially the parts that make us laugh the hardest, such as when a center steps nervously to the foul line for two shots, and his teammates cover their eyes, and the other team dons protective headgear, and children and dogs in the stands cower and weep, and even the referee, if you watch closely, edges away toward the other end of the court, while adamantly pretending he is not doing so; but he is.

A Passing Fancy

Sadly I did not learn to relish and savor the intricate creativity of passing a basketball to a teammate until the very end of my motley career; from the start I was a selfish and self-absorbed and solipsistic soul on the court, desiring only that I receive the ball as often as possible, ideally in my favorite spots, rather than delivering it with zest to another player in a position where *he* could do something with it. This was so even as my years as a ballplayer were also the years I watched some of the greatest passers in the history of the game at work night after night, visionaries who saw spaces and possibilities that no other player did, and who whipped the ball at incredible angles and speeds through those spaces, their passes very often leading to the easiest of baskets, or sometimes hitting the unprepared and deeply astonished recipient in the face. But even as I marveled at stunning passers, and was blessed with fine passers among my own teammates, it never occurred to me to join them in the selfless endeavor: no, my idea of an excellent game was one in which I received the ball regularly, ideally in my favorite spots, from which I could spin and score regularly, ideally in interesting and melodramatic ways; another one of my peculiar convictions on the court was that the degree of difficulty mattered greatly when you scored, and a basket coming at the end of a spectacularly unnecessary move was worth far more than an efficient and simple score. My friend Billy, the best point guard I ever played with, adamantly disagreed with me on this, and made his firm feelings known regularly and often rudely, sometimes right on the court, but who, I ask you, listens to a point guard?

Still, I admired terrific passing in theory, and enjoyed the deft pocket pass, and the perfectly timed backdoor pass, and the look-away pass, and the outlet pass, and the startling and dangerous crosscourt pass to an open shooter in the other corner, and the classic drive-and-dish pass that all good guards eventually mastered, and the wraparound pass by which a player aloft slipped the ball around his leaping defender and into the hands of a teammate, and the occasional brilliant sleight-of-hand pass, as when one player drives to the basket and at the last possible second flips the ball over his shoulder to a trailing player and how in the world did the first guy even *sense* that he had a teammate behind him, wow!

And the way a rebounder who could not get two hands on the ball but *could* get one hand on it would tip the ball to a teammate, and the wonderful touch pass, by which a player just gently redirects a pass with a flicker of fingers as it rockets by, and the occasional circus pass, as when a guy trapped by two defenders snaps a pass between the legs of one of the defenders, or bounces it between his own legs to a shooter behind him, and the occasional demoralizing full-court bounce pass to a streaking cutter for a layup, and the occasional spin pass by which the passer puts a tremendous spin on the ball as he lets it go, so that when it hits the floor it bounds away sharply at a wholly unexpected angle, ideally just as the smug defender is reaching for what seems like an easy steal; I saw this executed once so perfectly in a pickup game in Chicago that even as the passer's teammate caught the pass and laid the ball in the basket, both teams were laughing at the defender's aghast befuddlement, and the way he actually no-kidding stood there for a second staring at his hands, in which there was, amazingly, no basketball, although by all the laws of the universe it should have been *right there*.

I had to stop playing ball when I was about thirty, after various injuries, but in my last year, perhaps because I was slower and older, I began to see the flowing geometry of the game much better, and to notice how a generous passer could command a game without ever hardly scoring himself. I also noticed that a good passer seemed to make his teammates better without a word; they ran and cut harder, knowing that if they got open they would get the ball. I stopped playing before I ever got anywhere near to being a decent passer, let alone a good one, but I find that in the many years since I ceased to play my estimation and admiration for terrific passing has only continued to rise; perhaps I am slowly achieving a hint of maturity at last, and beginning to understand that generosity is the key to all great things—and basketball, invented one winter by an orphan from Ontario, is indisputably a great thing. It is instructive, by the way, to discover that in the very first game ever played, in Massachusetts, players were not allowed to dribble, run with, or kick the ball; the only way to advance it into scoring position was to pass.

A Day in Mayo

The only time I ever played a basketball game on grass was in the west of Ireland, on a blustery afternoon, me with my long lanky brothers against a quartet of burly local gentlemen, who were the most cheerful friendly young men you could imagine, airy and witty and headlong, though they were terrible basketball players. But they were, it turned out, excellent Gaelic football players, having been born and raised to love Peil Ghaelach, the ancient game invented by Cúchulainn and his friend Fergus many years ago in Armagh, when they were pitted against each other by a woman in a fight to the death, but *Is lesc lim-sa inní sin ám,* I am loath to do that, said Cúchulainn, and instead they invented the football, which we have played here ever since, said the young gentlemen, as they battered us here and there on the grass.

I have played ferocious rough ragged bruising games of basketball in New York City, and Chicago, and Boston, and in the Navajo Nation in New Mexico, but I never played in a rougher game than the one we played that bright sunny windy afternoon in Mayo. The young gentlemen had a decent grasp of the general idea of basketball, which is to put the ball through the basket and thus accumulate points and glory, but their approach was to ram the ball through the opposition to get as close to the goal as possible, and then try with might and main to put the ball in the basket, while fending off the opposition's herculean efforts to stop them from the aforementioned enterprise. Our herculean effort was mostly our oldest and widest brother Kevin, who was not only tall and burly but blessed with a stern and gruff mien, so that when two of the young gentlemen assailed him to move him out of the path of the approaching ball carrier, he growled and snarled and expostulated and caused them to pause long enough for the rest of us to arrive and set up a barrier, using our youngest brother Thomas as the point of the spear, or *na sleighe*, as one of the young gentlemen told me helpfully, noting that Cúchulainn carried a spear so famous that it had a name, the Gáe Bulga, which answered only to him, and was made from the bone of a sea monster, and was thrown interestingly with the foot and not the arm, and, once having entered its target, expanded therefrom into thirty spear points, so that it took a long time to reclaim it, after it had been the cause of chaos and mayhem.

I think now that my brothers and I won that game that day in Mayo, because our youngest brother Thomas was then in the full vigor of his youth, and was the best basketball player of all of us, and was tall and strong and could shrug off the young gentlemen, and also he could shoot the ball even when being heavily assailed, which my other brothers and I could not do; for us it was either shoot the ball or fend off assault, we could not do both at once; but Thomas could and did, and I have the vague memory that we won, because while the young gentlemen were skilled beyond belief at ramming the ball through us to get it to the basket, they could not hit the broad side of a barn with the ball, basically, and eventually the game ended because, as one of the young gentlemen told me, they had to be off to practice for the football, but they had much enjoyed the light skirmish, which they had found refreshing, and something like a casual warm-up for the rigorous demands of their own game, which had been played in Mayo for years beyond counting. We all shook hands happily, wiping away blood and mud. They invited us to their big match a few days later, against the dark forces of Donegal, but we had to decline, as we were due to return to America; and we all shook hands again, the young gentlemen approaching Mount Kevin with particular caution even then, and one of them said *Bhí sé ina onóir agus pléisiúr*, which I looked up later in an Irish dictionary: It has been an honor and a pleasure.

In the Alumni Gymnasium at
Dartmouth College Some Years Ago

I suppose it is silly to try to tell you the single greatest pass I ever saw on a basketball court, but why not pick one out from the many amazing passes I saw, so that we can all marvel at its subtle genius, and physical grace, and flash of magic, and almost unconscious brilliance, and make it a bright thread in the vast fabric of wonderful basketball passes, only a handful of which we sing and celebrate?

So, then, here we are, some years ago, on a beautiful gleaming court at Dartmouth College, in New Hampshire, not far from the Connecticut River. The river is frozen solid, and the little student gym we are in is freezing, but we are playing four on four full court, and the players are excellent, and the game is clean and fast, and we are working way too hard to be cold. It's one of those games where guys start playing harder and cutting sharper as the game goes on, because they are elevated by the quality of the play, and everyone ratchets up his game, and shots are dropping from impossible angles, and both teams are flying, and this game is going to come down to the last minute, which means that one or two key plays will be the difference, and so the rebounding wars are intense, and everyone is playing defense, even guys like me who hardly ever play defense, because this is a game you want to win, not for the victory—it's a Sunday morning pickup game against grad school guys we will never see again, who cares?—but because you all sense that this is about as good as it gets, as good as *you* get, as good as you and your friends can play, and you would be a dolt to waste a chance like this. It would be disrespectful to your boys, to yourself, to the profligate generosity of the game.

Then comes the pass. Our big center, seemingly a doughy guy but a terrific athlete and a crisp efficient ballplayer, sheds a couple of guys and grabs
a rebound. He's a smart young man, our center, and he knows without looking that his two guards should be off and sprinting the instant they see that
he is going to snag the rebound. He also knows that a free bucket here will
probably seal the game; he knows that if he can get rid of the ball in a hurry
we will have space in which to attack maybe only one startled defender;
so he pivots and cocks his arm and whips the ball like a baseball toward
where one of his guards should be. And indeed there is Billy drifting along
the sideline, angled in such a way that he can grab the outlet pass and snap
it right to me for a layup. But our center's pass is sailing—maybe he didn't
have his feet quite set, or he put too much spin on it, or he put too much
juice on it altogether, or the freezing gym is weirding out the flight of the
ball, because it's about to sail out of bounds, and probably smash through a
window and end up bouncing away down the river . . .

But our point guard leaps for it, floating over the sideline, and if you were
to slow this down and watch carefully you would realize slowly that he
doesn't want to catch it, or bat it back onto the court, or flip it gently over
his shoulder in hopes that a teammate might be cruising by. No: he just redirects it with the most gentle slight infinitesimal brush of his fingertips, so
that the ball rockets right to me, and I lay it in, and then there is the coolest
sound, as someone reaches down and helps Billy back to his feet—a whole
gym full of guys hooting and laughing at the most amazing pass they ever
saw. Of course both teams hooted and laughed. You would be a dolt not to
hoot and laugh at something so deftly done. You would be a fool not to savor
such a thing, whether or not it was your teammate who did it. Any guy who
makes a pass like that *is* your teammate, isn't that so?

The Guy Who Wore His Son
Like a Scarf

One time when I lived in Chicago I was playing basketball in a playground on the north side of the city when a tall guy wearing a little kid around his neck like a scarf showed up and called winners. Calling winners is claiming the right to play against the team that wins the game in progress. You can call winners even if you don't have any other guys to play with; you just pick and choose among guys who want to play. Usually you can claim most of the team that just lost, or pick from among guys on another court, or recruit from the local populace; I have seen guys who called winners recruit passersby, and guys hanging around the park with their girlfriends, and park employees, and one time a young priest (who was awful), and even once a kid on a swing, which sounds silly until I tell you the kid was terrific, a slippery little left-handed kid who knew how to survive among bigger players, and had the wit to pass the ball at every opportunity, which made his teammates like him, which led to him getting the ball back once in a while for shots of his own. Bright boy, that boy.

The tall guy with the kid wrapped around his neck watched our game closely, and he must have kept a sharp eye on the game on the adjacent court also, because when our game ended and he needed to pick three players, he quickly asked two guys from the other court and one from our court to play, and they said yes, and we all got ready to run. The tall guy very carefully unwrapped the kid from around his neck, and placed him gently on the bottom of the playground slide near the court, and then he took his jacket off, and wrapped the kid tightly in it, so that the kid looked like a hot dog in a bun, and then he hooked the sleeves of his jacket to the slide somehow, so the kid was sort of in the hammock of his jacket, and then we played ball. The tall guy was good, which was refreshing; often tall guys are just tall, and basketball is not their language, and half the time when you choose a tall guy as a sudden teammate you regret the choice after a couple of plays, and think bitterly how often height is wasted on tall guys who are awful at basketball.

We were playing four on four, full court to fifteen, and by happy chance the teams were evenly matched, and when the game was tied at thirteen we heard a high keening sound like a tiny siren. This was the kid, it turned out, who was making a high plaintive whimper like a nestling bird calling for its parents. And the tall guy, hearing this, stopped right in his tracks and said Sorry, guys, and walked off the court. We were a little annoyed; it's bad form to just bag out on a game. But there were eager guys waiting right there, and we picked one, and finished the game, and took a break.

No one said anything to the tall guy, who was unwrapping the kid, and then I happened to notice something, as I sprawled in the grass; the kid had no hands and feet. His arms and legs ended halfway to where his hands and feet should have been. He looked to be about two years old, a freckled friendly-looking little dude with hair that went seven ways at once. I would have laughed at the tumult of his hair but I was startled at seeing someone without hands and feet. The tall guy leaned the kid back on the slide, and put his jacket back on, and then he wrapped the kid around his neck like a scarf, and off they went down Fremont Street. I was supposed to get back on the court for the next game but I stood and watched them go for a while. The dad was walking in such a way that he deliberately jounced the kid up and down and I could hear the kid laughing all the way down to Cornelia Avenue. Sometimes even now when I hear a little kid laugh I hear that little kid laughing again all the way down to Cornelia Avenue.

The Mothers

One summer when I was in college my brothers and I played as a team in a summer league in New York. We called ourselves The Mothers for some reason I cannot remember. There were four of us and we would casually recruit a fifth guy on game days. Several times we recruited a friend on the way to the game, and once we recruited a guy about two minutes before our game started, plucking him from a pickup game in progress on the next court.

It was a highly entertaining basketball summer for all sorts of reasons. It was the summer that it became adamantly clear that our youngest brother, Tom, was by far the best of us, good enough to play in college. It was a summer-long tutorial by my brothers Kevin and Peter in hard work, and boxing out, and setting picks, and setting screens, and tipping rebounds if you couldn't get to them, and all the other subtle crucial aspects of ball that we do not talk about enough, fixated as we are on scoring and steals and blocked shots and flashy dribbling. It was the summer I finally achieved a trustworthy shot from either corner, after years of sloppy work. Also entertaining, at least to me, was the way that we were an utterly different team night to night depending on our fifth guy; one night we would have a banger, and be a team that attacked and defended the lane; another night we would have a quicksilver passer, and be a track team; another night we would have a guy who was a great athlete but not a basketball player, and anything could happen with a guy like that: he's a wild card, capable of a terrific play followed instantly by a terrible play, and you have no idea which will be when. I found that I was even more alert than usual when our fifth guy was a guy like that, because he was a chaos agent, and there were more loose balls available for me to convert into shots.

But the highlight of the summer for me was a game at the end of August. I disremember anything about the other team other than they wiped us out right from the start. They were tall and fast and talented and merciless and within minutes they were up by ten, and then twenty, and then thirty, and so on, and as I remember they beat us by some ridiculous margin, like fifty or sixty points. This sounds like it should be embarrassing and humiliating, but it wasn't, partly because they were just so inarguably better, and partly for the thing I will remember the rest of my life: near the end of the game, even though we were down by fifty or so, my brothers were working their asses off. My brother Tom, who had been double-teamed the entire game, was still whipping passes through the crowd and driving to the basket while wearing one or two defenders, and my brother Kevin, who was big and slow and grim and relentless, was still banging away in the lane for rebounds, and my brother Peter, tall and lean and grim, was still unfolding like a derrick to block careless shots, and I was still trying every cut I knew to get open long enough to receive a bullet pass from Tom for a decent shot. On one play, I remember, I drifted out into the corner and rested for a moment, exhausted, hands on knees, watching my three brothers storm the citadel yet again, though we had long ago lost the battle. Just for an instant, for a second or two before I jumped back into the fray, I realized that what they were doing was wholly and wordlessly admirable, that they were refusing to quit no matter what the score, that they were playing the game as it should be played no matter what the odds, and I was deeply inarticulately proud of them, and filled with love, and I never knew how to say that enough then or for years afterward, but now I do. Now I do.

Covering Chris

For several years when I was youngish I played one-on-one full-court basketball twice a week against a friend named Chris. We played in a tiny gym on the fourth floor of the ancient dilapidated creaking Young Men's Christian Union building on Boylston Street, on the edge of Chinatown. Games were to fifteen by ones, you had to win by two baskets, best two of three games wins: we would lock the gym door behind us so as not to have to deal with interlopers, and as well as being exhilaratingly physically exhausting, these were among the most intense complex intellectually strenuous games of my peculiar basketball career, for we knew each other so well, knew each other's predilections and preferences and habits and customs so thoroughly, that the games became not only athletic contests but high-speed chess games. So come with me into one of those games, and let us delve into covering Chris, which was an adventure, as he was six inches taller, and could shoot, and was the most ferociously competitive guy I ever met.

But I was quick, and devious, and could jump, and was utterly willing to hold and jostle and shove and touch his elbow ever so gently when he went up for a shot so that he would miss but not be quite absolutely sure he had been fouled, and things like that, so we were fairly evenly matched; so it came down to decisions like this:

It's his ball. I crowd him just enough so that he cannot just sit there in the rocking chair and hit a set shot, but not so much that he has the urge to drop his shoulder and drive. I know he wants to get closer to the basket; tall guys are shorter the farther away they are from the hole. But as soon as he starts his dribble, the ball is down where I can poke and slap and swipe at it; any time he brings the ball down below his waist, it's my ball, is my theory. He knows this, so he turns halfway before backing down, to protect the ball. But now I can hide in his blind spot and snap at the ball; or, because I know he knows this and hates me stealing him blind like that, I hint that way and jump the other way, right into his path. But, ah! He is no fool, and he's already spun the other way, to the spot I just vacated, and he hits the short jumper.

My ball. I start with a rocker step, to keep him unbalanced. He knows I want to drive to his left, with my right hand; I have no left hand to speak of. But I know he knows my weakness, so I am just as liable to drive hard to his right side, and either pull up sharply for a sudden jumper, or crossover dribble instantly back to my strong hand, and either drive or pull up there, as he staggers a little to get back into the play. Or I can drive hard to either side and then instantly step back for a shot, or, as soon as he steps out to contest the shot, fly by him for a layup. Or, as occasionally happens, even though it's a low-percentage shot, I can just suddenly shoot the ball from where I stand, if I think he's ever so slightly lower in his defensive stance

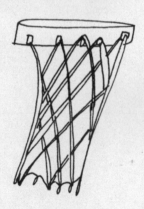

than he should be. But this time the calculation is that he's giving too much room to my strong hand; I can tell that he's inviting me to go that way, gently suggesting it, opening the gate, trying to cut down the possibilities by shepherding me that way; and he has also gauged, correctly, that I would rather drive than shoot the jumper, as I am not a great shooter; but I understand all of his subtle calculations just from the angle of his feet, and decide, essentially without thinking, to jab-step to his right side, which will force him to move his feet slightly, and then go as hard as possible back through the gate he's left ajar; which I do, and get right to the basket; but he has recovered swiftly, and is coming to block the layup, so I just keep going under the basket, and flip the ball in off the backboard, calculating, correctly, that he will not be able to reach it, as tall guys often get hampered by the net.

All of this, these two baskets, took maybe twenty seconds. So imagine the intricate exhilarating exhausting chess of, say, eighty baskets; and you will understand why, even today, when I think of those games in that tiny sweltering gym, I start to laugh, and feel younger for a moment, and remember how, even when I lost those games, I totally utterly absolutely inarguably won those games.

Dunking

I did actually, no kidding, really and truly, with witnesses present, dunk
a regulation basketball, a Spalding, as I recall, during a full-court game
in Boston, on a sunny day, many years ago, on a court on the banks of the
Charles River. I did that. Men on both teams saw me do that, although there
is no film, or written account of the event, other than this note. There *were*
some extenuating circumstances. The basket was inarguably two inches
low. I had been a total slacker on defense, taking every opportunity to leak
out on the break and receive outlet passes from teammates and get the
right angle on the basket and get my footwork right and sail in with just the
right combination of factors such that I could actually no-kidding maybe
dunk. It was my ball and I knew it well and we were friendly and it fit my
hand and I knew how to slam the last dribble hard to get a tiny bit more ele-
vation. I had tried to dunk on this exact basket fifty times so I knew the rim
about as well as you can know a rim on which you have banged your wrist
fifty times and one time nearly lost a finger in the metal-mesh net when
my finger snagged for an instant as the rest of me was returning to Mother
Earth. I had swept the court beforehand to be sure there were no pebbles
or shards of glass underfoot as I attempted to actually no-kidding really
and truly dunk. I was wearing exactly the right sneakers, new enough to be
supportive but worn enough to be comfortable. I was twenty-six years old,
just the right age for this moment, young enough to be supple and bouncy
but old enough to be disciplined and plan the attack. I had not one but three
mountainous teammates to rebound and get me the ball on the break. I
had one other teammate who was invested in the attempt because he had

money riding on a negative outcome, and money is excellent motivation for getting me the ball on the break as often as possible so that there would be no quibble about the number of chances I had been given by my teammates during the game. The weather was fine, the opposing team good enough to whet our competitive juices but poor enough to give up lots of rebounds and outlet passes to me on the break. There were no spectators to hiss at me or cast aspersions or offer insulting and unjust remarks. There were no park officials to remind me that there was ABSOLUTELY NO DUNKING OR HANGING ON RIMS on the courts in the park. The sun was not behind the basket I was assaulting. It was high hot summer so that we were all loose and rubbery and leapish. And leap I did, with every ounce of bounce in me, and I had gauged my steps correctly, and had a good grip on the ball, and up I went, as high as I could, and I just managed to squeak the ball over the rim by what must have been a zillionth of an inch, but it was inarguably and incontestably a dunk, and I would have hung on the rim for a second or two to show off, but I was so startled that I had actually dunked that I came down awkwardly and nearly fell down, but I staggered up and trotted back to the other end of the court, grinning from ear to ear. I didn't *say* anything, or crow, or shout, or pretend to be an airplane, or skip, or swagger, or thump my chest, or cup my ears for applause, because to do those things would have been totally uncool, but I *was* grinning ear to ear as I arrived back among my teammates, who seemed to have missed the epic event, because none of them said anything for a minute, and then our center said *Now* are you going to play defense? Did you get it out of your system? Because you have been a total candyass on defense so far, and we could use some help here, man. My other teammates laughed and I tracked down the guy I was supposed to be covering and the game rolled on, and afterwards I said What a day, right? and our center said Yup, great game, I think we won by maybe ten.

There's Lots of Other Stuff to See
if You Look Real Close

Weirdly enough, the guy who probably taught me the most about how to use my entire body as a sensory device on a basketball court was a guy with only one eye. This was in a schoolyard playground in Chicago many years ago. He was a tall reedy guy of indeterminate ethnic background although people called him Yang for some reason. He didn't look noticeably Asian to me but names are fluid things on basketball courts; I would guess half the guys I played with over the years were addressed by names other than the ones their parents gave them. If I close my eyes and concentrate I can still see guys called Dud, and Four, and Fat, and T, and many other odd handles and labels and adjectives like that.

He was skinny but strong, this guy, and he was a very good ballplayer, always one of the first guys picked when teams were being composed. I think because he and I were whitish, among many players who were brownish, that we were often thrown together on teams, so we got to be sort-of-friends in the basketball way, which is that you communicate well without words on court, and chat casually off court while waiting to be on court again. One time, though, after a long great afternoon of ball, as guys wandered off, Yang and I stayed on court, and he conducted an impromptu clinic for me about spacing, and using your hands to keep track of where guys were, and how you could feel defenders with your butt, and how you could see in three directions at once if you didn't focus on one direction, and how you could sense what play might develop just from the way guys ran; you could almost always tell which way the ball would go on a fast break, for example, by watching the wing men, not the ball handler. The ball handler, he said, is in the illusion business, whereas the cutters have to commit to an idea before the ball handler does; so I watch the cutters, and every third time or so you jump the pass. Not every time. Same thing with picks; if you watch the guy setting the pick, he'll almost always tell you if the ball handler is going to use the pick or not. Guys who set picks *hate* it when the ball handler doesn't use the pick, and they set shoddy lazy picks because of that, so you can jump the ball handler, who is shocked when you are right where he wanted to be hoisting his open shot.

The best place to figure out where everyone is going is in the lane when it's crowded, he continued. You don't *hold* anyone, but you keep your hands awake. I keep one hand on the guy I am covering and keep the other hand open for news. My guy suddenly whips around, I know he expects the ball. My guy suddenly crowds me, I know he's trying to move me off the play. He extends his arms, I figure there's a shot up and he's setting up to rebound. And the lane is a great space for your butt to be paying attention. I can *feel* a guy crossing the lane in a hurry behind me, and if he's in a hurry that probably means the play is for him, you know?

Little things like that, man, he concluded. You can score, I seen that all summer, but you don't see shit on defense. I only have the one eye so maybe I have to look harder, you know? But it's all there if you look sharp. *You* just react to stuff, and hoop is so fast that reacting to stuff is mostly too late. You see obvious stuff, like which hand a guy prefers, and what are his patterns, does he go for pump fakes, does he like to pass, does he hate to drive, can he *only* drive, stuff like that, but there's lots of other stuff to see if you look real close, you know? OK? We good? See you tomorrow, man. Good game today. That was a real good run.

West Side

One time when I lived in Chicago I wandered to the West Side of the city in search of a good pickup game of basketball. My usual haunts were courts on the North Side but for various excellent reasons I had to take a sabbatical from the North Side, and the South Side entailed a train or a bus, but the West Side was close enough to dribble into, and to my delight I found a great park on Montrose Avenue, with serious games with serious players. I played all afternoon at this park—Horner Park, which used to be a brick factory and was named for Illinois's first Jewish governor—and then wandered home in the early evening, happily exhausted.

It was a long walk from Montrose back to my apartment by the lake, and I stopped along the way for a beer in one of those classic unadorned corner bars that were and probably still are quiet features of the city's ethnic neighborhoods—many of them called simply Dan's or Joe's or Pete's, some without names at all, and all of them that I remember utterly unflashy; they looked a lot like the houses crowded around them, and I always had the sense that they were places where people would just pop in for a beer on the way home, or on a Saturday afternoon; the sort of place that would hold a wake for a respected late neighbor, and sponsor a softball team, and shell out happily to outfit the local Little League team. The corner bar . . . along with the diner, and the library, and the post office, and the firehouse, and the grade school, what could be more urban American than the unassuming corner bar?

As I got my beer, though, I heard a thumping sound behind the bar, and out back I found a kid and a bedraggled hoop without a net. Somebody had nailed a homemade backboard to the wall of the bar years ago, and apparently abandoned it ever after; you never saw such a sorry amalgam of battered backboard, rusting hoop, and ancient ball in your life. The kid, though, was drilling his shots, and after a minute, in the eternal way of basketball, he asked me if I wanted to play, without saying anything, and I said yes, without saying anything, and put my beer down on a rickety picnic table, and we played horse for a while. Horse is an old shooting game during which one guy makes a shot and the other guy has to match the exact shot; if you miss, you get a letter, and the guy who spells *horse* first loses.

Now, I was a decent shooter then, good enough to hit half my shots, usually; but this kid was killing me, and he was all of maybe twelve years old. He could hit every shot I tried, and I could match him up to the point where he shot bank shots; there he lost me, for reasons that took me a while to figure out. Finally he pointed out to me that the backboard was weirdly curved by age and rain and winter; but even after that I struggled to play the angles on it, while he continued to drop one bank shot after another cleanly through the hoop.

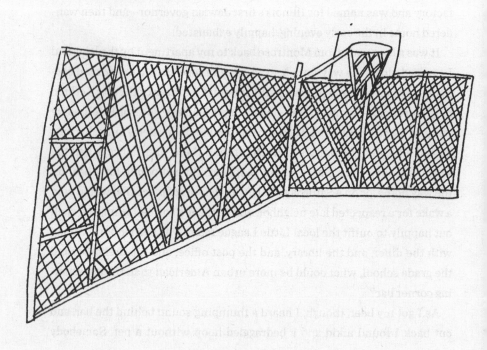

A minute later two burly young guys came out of the bar and challenged us to play two on two. For a while the game was clean and fun and then something changed and the young guys got rougher. I had just been cruising, having played all day, but I got annoyed and tried to buckle down and carry the game, but it turned out I was out of gas. I had been passing dutifully to the kid before, but now I gave him the ball every time, and just set hard screens for him to get his shot off, and it still makes me happy to remember him drilling one impossible bank shot after another, against testy beery burly guys who were a foot taller and getting angrier by the minute. Finally he hit one from way out and the burly guys stomped back inside and the kid and I shook hands and I left my beer on the table for him, which sounds like a stupid thing to do, to leave a beer for a twelve-year-old kid, but I felt, and still feel, that it was somehow a gesture of respect. I know that sounds weird, but he and I both knew what the gesture meant, and you do, too. It was just a beer, but it wasn't just a beer. It was a way to say to the kid I see all those hours you've shot here alone, figuring out every millimeter of this soggy old backboard, all the hours you've spent walking here and back from your house or your apartment, all the hours in the rain and the snapping cold, all the times people barked at you from the bar and nearby houses, all the times you spun and hit a long fall-away from deep in the corner at the buzzer and won the game because I was you, too, little brother, I was you, too, and I still am, somehow, somewhere, somehow.

The Skinny Guy

I was privileged once to see a small-not-small moment that meant the world to six young men but nothing at all to anyone else; I was only apprised of it by chance, before the basketball game, by a guy on the other team who knew I was a story junkie and would be interested.

See the skinny guy with the cast on his wrist? he said. He's off to the Navy tomorrow at dawn. He signed up for the whole nine yards. Eight years. All the guys in his family are Navy. This is his last game ever with us. We have all played together since third grade. Every single year, winter and summer league. Just us six. We made a pact. But this is it. We all grew up together within three streets. We ate so much at the other guys' houses that the moms put an extra chair at the table for whichever of us was eating over. It was always hoop for us. I mean we played football and baseball and lacrosse and stuff but it was always hoop first. We invented our own drills. We had one drill that was just up and down the court as fast as you can, passing to each other as fast as you can. We figured that we would never be the *best* six guys but we could be in the best shape. Also, no prima donnas. We policed ourselves. Two guys are better than the rest but those two are the best passers. The skinny guy is probably the worst of us. Great guy, though. He'll get leave sometimes and we'll play when he is home but this is the last night of the old days. After this we are just guys who might see each other here and there, you know? So watch what happens. I bet something cool happens that you would have to know the story to see why it's cool, you know what I mean?

I did know what he meant and I watched for it. When the game began I thought it was that the guy was a starter, even though he wasn't that good, not to mention the cast. But that wasn't it. Then once when I was sitting on our bench catching my breath and watching the other team closely I noticed that his friends were ever so smoothly covering for him on defense; whenever he was in the wrong spot, or lost his guy, one of his teammates slid over and hid his mistake without fanfare. But the more I watched the more I concluded that the skinny guy was just a poor defender, and his friends were used to it, and probably they'd always covered for him.

Then late in the game I saw it. My team was up by ten with about five minutes to play, and since this was the end of summer league, with no play-offs, the game downshifted a little, and we just cruised up and down to finish cleanly and not let it slip away. The skinny guy hit a little hook, and then a tough layup, and something woke me up, and I watched with interest as every single time the other team got the ball in those last minutes they fed the skinny guy. They didn't make a big deal of it, and no one high-fived or anything like that, but he took probably their last ten shots in a row, and hit half of them, too, even wearing a cast.

The game ended and we all shook hands and wandered off to our cars arguing about where to get a beer. I stood for a minute watching the other team. The skinny guy was in the middle as they walked to their cars and his teammates kept gently slapping his head and bumping him off-stride with their shoulders and they were all laughing and something about the way they jostled him and slapped his head so gently was moving and eloquent. I watched them arrive at their cars and just as the skinny guy was about to fold himself into the shotgun seat of one of the cars a teammate jumped in front of him and slammed the door and the cars peeled away with the skinny guy running behind them shouting and very faintly you could hear them all laughing.

Otters v. Counselors

Probably the funniest basketball game I ever played in was the Senior Camp Counselors versus the Otters, the Otters being kids five and six years old in their first summer at the camp high on a hill over Long Island Sound, so high that you could indeed see Connecticut on clear days, sprawled on the horizon like a long green dab of paint. One of the Otters, in fact, a silent boy named Aram, actually lived in Connecticut, and was driven to and from camp every morning in, I kid you not, an enormous town car with a massive driver in a meticulous black suit. I asked Aram once what he did during the drive, which must have been almost two hours each way, and he said mostly he slept, but sometimes he and the driver played games having to do with spotting license plates, and the colors of cars, and counting the number of other drivers smoking cigarettes, and noting the species of birds spotted along the road, and remembering the best meals they had ever had; the driver was from Trinidad and Tobago, said Aram, and mostly his, the driver's, favorite meals had to do with fish stuffed with fruit.

Aram was one of the Otters, as were a slew of other spindly boys whose faces come back to me now when I see their names before me in books and newspapers and on billboards and street signs: Elijah and Isaiah, Jesus and James, Aaron and Adam. I remember once giving a speech to the Otters, as we were preparing for swimming lessons, about the remarkably biblical cast of their nomenclature, the primarily desert provenance of their given names; how rare and lovely to find a room full of young men bearing the names of legendary characters from that one tumultuous region of the world, eh, boys? And I well remember the way they stared at me with not the slightest idea what I was saying, as usual. It was Aram who once said to me, by the archery pit, that he and the other Otters often wondered if *I* knew what I was talking about when I delivered one of my speeches, which still seems to me an excellent question.

The senior counselors versus the first-years was a camp tradition, attended by not only all campers and staff but many parents and families. It was held late in the afternoon of the last day, and was followed by an awards ceremony and picnic. As the senior senior counselor that year, I got to handpick my team of counselors (for entertainment, I chose all those who had never played basketball), and also arranged the Otters into groups of five, to be shuttled in and out every few minutes, so that they would all get to play, even Aram, who was so scared of the ball that I had let him sit under a tree and doze during Basketball Hour all summer.

The court was at the very top of the hill, and it was a hot windy day, and the stands were packed, and the game was hilarious, and no one got hurt or embarrassed, and the Counselors racked up probably fifty turnovers, so that the Otters, playing as hard as they could, won the game by four points, although the final score was something like ten to six. And while I vividly remember Aram's face when he hoisted up a shot and I accidentally tipped it in for him, it is the ripples and tides and swirls and eddies of laughter on that windy hot summer afternoon that I remember best now; the way the Otters giggled helplessly, and the way the Counselors, each of us trying to play worse than the others, laughed so hard that our cheeks and bellies hurt for days afterward, and how Aram's driver, in his shining suit, leaning up against the shining town car, laughed so uproariously, so un-self-consciously, that his cap tipped back and, as I watched, fell off; but he reached back smoothly and caught it with one hand, and a few minutes later, as he welcomed Aram into their car for their last ride home, he looked over at me and tipped his cap, a lovely and subtle gesture that I hope I never forget, as long as I live.

The Niece

And speaking of coaching, I was once coached, in a manner of speaking, by a child of seven, a girl, the niece of a friend of mine, before and during a summer league game, against a bitter rival, in Boston, some years ago, under towering elms so big and broad that when the sun declined behind them late in the afternoon the court lights went on automatically because of the dark.

We didn't have a coach, to speak of, that summer; what instruction and motivation we occasionally needed came from our superb point guard, who would murmur something intelligent as he dribbled past, or suggest casually that we switch defenses, or even positions; although just as often he would call us together in a huddle and ask where we should go get a beer after the game. He was also fond of asking sidelong questions during time-outs, an entertaining habit; once I remember him in the huddle offering five bucks on the spot to anyone who could name the entire twelve-man roster of the 1970 New York Knicks. I came close, missing only Bill Hosket, but unbelievably our backup point guard, who hardly ever spoke at all, suddenly rattled off the entire team, *complete with their uniform numbers, in ascending numerical order*, from number 5, Don May, to number 33, Cazzie Russell, and including the often-forgotten rookie John Warren, number 19. He tucked the fiver in his shorts. We were so amused at this that we had to call a second time-out, much to the annoyance of the referee.

It was the last game that summer that the kid coached us. Our power forward's sister had left the kid with him for the weekend while she went off with a new boyfriend with whom she had hopes, and our friend couldn't very well leave the kid in his apartment. His idea was to have her sit on our bench just so he could keep an eye on her during the game, so down she plopped on the bench before the game, next to our point guard, and soon they were in a serious discussion about whether we should try a box-and-one defense against the other team's star shooter, or just try to outscore the bastards, as the kid phrased it. Our point guard was all for the box-and-one, but the kid said that from what she had heard if we were on our game and in full flow it would be harder for them to stop us than otherwise, so we started out in our standard man-to-man.

Their shooter was killing us, though, and after a while the kid called a time-out and said OK, fine, try the box if you want, but every third time down switch into a straight tight double-team just to rattle him. Also, *someone* needs to come up and set a high pick on offense. And stop dribbling so much. *Move* the ball.

The switching defenses did rattle that shooter, and we clicked into gear in the second half and pulled away and won by ten. We needed the win, too, because it meant the second seed, and no one that summer wanted any part of the top seed, a team of firefighters who were all in terrific shape and loved to run; playing them was like playing a track team. We knew we would probably face them in the final, and just for fun, after the game, we asked the niece what she would suggest defensively if we made the title game, and she said, memorably, Well, basically you are screwed, but if you attack the boards and leave both guards back on defense, you have a slim chance. Even if you play well you'll probably lose by ten, but you have a chance if the guards stay back to slow down their break.

Indeed we did face the firefighters in the final, and we did as she said, and I have to say that we gave them all they could handle, but they were relentless and there seemed to be waves of them, all young and crew-cut and muscles, and we lost by eight. I still think we played them as well as anyone could have played them that summer, though, so in that sense it was a victory.

Laughing and Jigging and Laughing

It may not be the case that every basketball team had or has a warm-up song, but I played on a team in Boston that *did* have one—"Naive Melody," by the Talking Heads—and this morning I would like to press the play button on a big battered paint-splattered boom box on the third floor of a sagging moist ancient wooden unkempt Boston three-flat, on the west side of the city, on a hot sweltering summer evening, just as the sun is heading home from work, and let's watch as most of the guys on that team, who are sprawled lazily here and there in the ratty kitchen, all long legs and long hair and old sneakers, sit up smiling as the music takes hold, and some part of each of those guys gets it that it's game time, boys, time to gear up, let's be ready to run!

> Feet on the ground, head in the sky
> It's OK, I know nothing's wrong, nothing
> I got plenty of time

And the guy who pressed play on his old boom box starts to jig and caper, and a second guy, the excellent point guard, who is also painting houses between jobs, which is why the boom box is all speckled with paint, he jumps up and starts jigging a little, too, which makes two other guys laugh and jump up and start jigging, and then the other three guys in the kitchen cannot resist the adamant silliness of all this, and they start jigging, also, and one of these guys is a serious large burly guy with a chest so broad it has its own zip code and telephone exchange, and now the old thin floor is shaking noticeably, and probably shedding a few paint flakes on the residents below, who sometimes no-kidding bang broom handles against the ceiling to tell us to shut up and turn that music down!, but not this time, maybe because they dig the song, also, because who doesn't dig this song?, this is the most irresistible catchy goofy pop song ever, the exact right song to get into the mood for a summer game outdoors under the elms in the park, man, let's go!

> The less we say about it the better
> Make it up as we go along

So here are seven guys in their twenties, all sorts and sizes and shapes, laughing and jigging in the kitchen as they slowly get into their hoop gear and find sneakers and borrow socks, and two guys are spray-painting the team logo on their shirts because as usual we never got around to getting regular uniforms and instead spray paint onto shirts through a stencil that one of us cut through cardboard with a steak knife.

> There was a time before we were born
> If someone asks, this is where I'll be, where I'll be

And in a minute we will be jigging down the long narrow winding stairs past graffiti on the walls, graffiti that to be honest we were responsible for but let's not get into that just now, for just now we are jigging down the staircase and the music is booming off the old wooden walls and we are into it, man, we are awake and alert and aligned and eager and ready, and in a minute we will pile into old cars and head to the park, but just now the Heads are wrapping up that bright cheerful goofy merry song that their bassist has said smiling was born with a loose laughing jam in which all the members of their team were jigging and shucking and bopping as they played, and they just kept jazzing and bouncing because it was so much genuine honest unadorned fun to be on the same page in the same moment in the same happy goofy mood, which is exactly how we felt in that kitchen on those summer evenings, and also why, every time I have ever heard that song in the many years since I was in that kitchen, I am immediately back in that hot summer kitchen again, laughing and jigging and laughing.

My Seventy Thousandth Foul

Knocked over a small child the other day, by accident. He was prancing around down by my shins, and I had not seen him, and I turned sharply for some reason, and knocked him sprawling. I hasten to report that he was not hurt, and he bounced up giggling, and I apologized profusely, and he fell down again for amusement's sake, and he and I laughed immoderately, and the world spun on in its ancient custom, but the thought occurred to me later, as I counted up the fouls I had committed in life, that this may well have been my seventy thousandth foul, and *seventy thousand* is a remarkable epic alpine number that should be celebrated, and pondered, and gaped at, as you would gawk at a Republican in a dashiki.

I played basketball pretty much every day from age nine to age thirty, and while there were some days when I could only get in an hour of ball, there were many days when I played for two hours easy, and there were some glorious and memorable summers when I played two hours during the day and a whole summer-league game at night. The cold fact of the matter is that I was a terrible defensive player from the start, and never got any better, even as I grew taller and quicker and fell head over teakettle in love with the intricate joys of the game; also I had the poor defender's inordinate urge to swipe at the ball, and try for steals and blocked shots even when there was no conceivable way you could steal or reject the ball without hammering the ball handler or the shooter; and finally I much enjoyed collisions, and set picks and screens with cheerful vehemence, and dove into scrums with reckless abandon, and no man ever more enjoyed the thicket of bristling elbows and not especially surreptitious shoves as players wrestled and jostled for rebounding position.

All of which is to say that I committed far more than my share of fouls, in every imaginable venue and aspect of the game: holding on to bigger faster players with one quiet hand, two if they were burly centers; grabbing shirts and jerseys and shorts; shoving opponents out of bounds with a subtle knee or hip, knowing full well that the referee's eyes would be on the ball; happily greeting an opponent with a forearm to the throat as he drove the lane; cracking at a ball handler's forearm to loosen his grip on the ball; leaping for a blocked shot and crashing gleefully into the shooter with no regret; reaching around a ball handler who had half-driven past me, and snapping at the ball from behind to try to poke it out, and smacking the ball handler instead; leaping to contest a shot, and ever so gently hitting the shooter's proffered elbow instead of going for the ball; this last a surpassing art when done well, as by, for example, my brother Tommy, a master of the craft. He was also a genius at gently shoving you away from the basket with one hand while contesting your shot with his innocent other hand, so that while you thought you were pulling up for an easy jump shot from ten feet away, soon you were, to your surprise, shooting a fall-away fifteen-footer, a much different proposition.

I figure that I committed probably nine fouls a day, every day, for twenty-one years, for a round total of roughly sixty-nine thousand fouls. If we add in the days when I was really on my game, foul-wise, or had significant extra opportunities, like those games in a narrow cement alley with my huge intent muscular vengeful brothers, plus the fouls I committed on defenders when *I* had the ball, we approach seventy thousand. Let us assume, as well we should, that I committed any number of personal fouls off the court—on the soccer field, in romantic tilts, in the course of writing novels, in the corporate jungle, in the automobile, on tax forms—and we can type the number *seventy thousand* with confidence, or rue, or wince, or grin; or all of the above.

His Last Game

We were supposed to be driving to the pharmacy for his prescriptions but he said just drive around for a while, my prescriptions aren't going anywhere without me, so we just drove around. We drove around the edges of the college where he had worked and we saw a blue heron in a field of stubble, which is not something you see every day, and we stopped for a while to see if the heron was fishing for mice or snakes, on which we bet a dollar, me taking mice and him taking snakes, but the heron glared at us and refused to work under scrutiny, so we drove on.

We drove through the arboretum checking on the groves of ash and oak and willow trees, which were still where they had been last time we looked, and then we checked on the wood duck boxes in the pond, which still seemed sturdy and did not feature ravenous weasels that we noticed, and then we saw a kestrel hanging in the crisp air like a tiny helicopter, but as soon as we bet mouse or snake the kestrel vanished, probably for religious reasons, said my brother, probably a *lot* of kestrels are adamant that gambling is immoral, but we are just *not* as informed as we should be, in the end, about kestrels.

We drove farther and I asked him why we were driving this direction and he said I am looking for something that when I see it you will know what I am looking for, which made me grin, because he knew and I knew that I would indeed know, because we have been brothers for fifty years, and brothers have many languages, some of which are physical, like broken noses and fingers and teeth and punching each other when you want to say I love you but don't know how to say that right, and some of them are

194

laughter, and some of them are roaring and spitting, and some of them are weeping in the bathroom, and some of them we don't have words for yet.

By now it was almost evening, and just as he turned on the car's running lights I saw what it was he was looking for, which was a basketball game in a park. I laughed and he laughed and we pulled over. There were six guys on the court and to their credit they were playing full court. Five of the guys looked to be in their twenties and they were fit and muscled and one of them wore a porkpie hat. The sixth guy was much older but he was that kind of older ballplayer who is comfortable with his age and he knew where to be and what not to try.

We watched for a while and didn't say anything but both of us noticed that one of the young guys was not as good as he thought he was, and one was better than he knew he was, and one was flashy but essentially useless, and the guy with the porkpie hat was a worker, setting picks, boxing out, whipping outlet passes, banging the boards not only on defense but on offense, which is much harder. The fifth young guy was one of those guys who ran up and down yelling and waving for the ball, which he never got. This guy was supposed to be covering the older guy but he didn't bother and the older guy gently made him pay for his inattention, scoring occasionally on backdoor cuts and shots from the corners on which he was so alone he could have opened a circus and sold tickets, as my brother said.

The older man grew visibly weary as we watched, and my brother said he's got one last basket in him, and I said I bet a dollar it's a shot from the corner, and my brother said no, he doesn't even have the gas for that, he'll snake the kid somehow, you watch, and just then the older man, who was bent over holding the hems of his shorts like he was exhausted, suddenly cut to the basket, caught a bounce pass, and scored, and the game ended, maybe because the park lights didn't go on even though the streetlights did.

On the way home my brother and I passed the heron in the field of stubble again, and the heron stopped work again and glared at us until we turned the corner.

That is one *withering* glare, said my brother. That's a ballplayer glare if ever I saw one. That's the glare a guy gives another guy when the guy you were supposed to be covering scores on a backdoor cut and you thought your guy was ancient and near death but it turns out he snaked you good and you are an idiot. *I* know that glare. You owe me a dollar. We better go get my prescriptions. They are not going to do any good but we better get them anyway so they don't go to waste. One less thing for my family to do afterward. That game was good but the heron was even better. We already paid for the prescriptions so we might as well get them. They'll just get thrown out if we don't pick them up. That was a good last game, though. I'll remember the old guy, sure, but the kid with the hat banging the boards, that was cool. You hardly ever see a guy with a porkpie hat hammering the boards. There's so much to love. All the little things. Remember shooting baskets at night and the only way you could tell if the shot went in was the sound of the net? Remember the time we cut the fingertips off our gloves so we could shoot on icy days and dad was so angry he lost his voice and he was supposed to give a speech and had to gargle and mom laughed so hard we thought she was going to pee? Remember that? I remember that. What happens to what I remember? You remember it for me, okay? You remember the way that heron glared at us like he would kick our asses except he was working. And you remember that old man snaking that kid. *Stupid kid*, you could say, but that's the obvious thing. The *beautiful* thing is the little thing that the old guy knew full well he wasn't going to cut around picks and drift out into the corner again, that would burn his last gallon of gas, not to mention he would have to hoist up a shot from way out there, so he snakes the kid beautiful, he knows the kid thinks he's old, and the guy with the hat sees him cut, and gets him the ball on a dime, that's a beautiful thing because it's little, and we saw it and we knew what it meant. You remember that for me. You owe me a dollar.

The Young Woman

Some years ago I was working as an editor and writer at a college magazine when the college welcomed the most famous women's basketball recruit in its long history. This young woman was six feet tall and unbelievably quick and deft and confident on the court. She had been an All-American at a local high school. She had obliterated the state scoring record. She would become the only player, male or female, ever to be All-American all four years of her career at the college. She would go on to play professionally. And this was the person I challenged to a game one afternoon in the college gym. We would play three games to fifteen. The college photographer would capture some moments. I would write a piece for the magazine, and so introduce the young woman to the magazine's readership. It would be a different approach, I thought, not the usual profile or article or puff piece.

The quiet young woman was amenable to this odd idea. We shook hands as we warmed up. I tried not to look as she drilled almost every one of the hundred shots she told me she shot as her regular warm-up. Every shot was taken with the exact same form, and every shot that went in seemed to drop through the exact center of the basket, snapping the net in such a way that the ball bounced back to her for her next shot.

We began. I tried every shot and move and fake and hitch and stutter step and pivot and spin and reverse spin in my repertoire, and I was a decent ballplayer with many thousands of hours of experience in leagues and courts and gyms from New York to Chicago to Boston. I thought I was good. I had no illusions; I knew my ceiling, I knew I wasn't *very* good, I knew there were many better players than me; but it was very clear, very quickly, that this young woman, all of nineteen years old, was very, very good, and she beat me without, it seemed to me, undue effort. She hit any shot she wanted, from any spot on the floor, and when she wanted to drive to the basket she drove with authority, with either hand. I tried cutting her off, I tried swiping at the ball, I tried to block her shot, but nothing availed, and she won each of the three games easily. I didn't get crushed, quite; I played respectably; but within the first two minutes it was clear that there was a superb basketball player on the floor, and then there was me.

You would think that a guy who absolutely loved the game and had poured so many hours into it, a guy who was a decent ballplayer with decent athletic skills and thousands of hours of honing his game, would be annoyed, or embarrassed, or angry, or humiliated, or something other than what I was, but I was, somehow, oddly, delighted. One of the best things about basketball is that it is an inarguable sport; if someone is better than you, then he, or she, is better than you, and that's that. She was *much* better than me, and by the end of our games I found myself marveling at her economy of motion, her unshakable confidence, her amazing accuracy; you had the feeling that she could take a thousand shots at any basket in the world and most of those shots would drop through the exact center of the basket, snapping the net in such a way that the ball bounced back to her for the next shot.

I knew, vaguely, that women's basketball was changing and growing and booming in remarkable ways then; I knew it had come far from the days when players wore skirts and played six on six; but I had never imagined that women's basketball had such astonishing excellence in it, a player of such grace and strength and calm mastery.

We shook hands, smiling, and then we went our ways, me to write my story and the young woman to go to class, as I recall; but as I walked back to my office I found myself moved. I couldn't quite articulate it then, but now I think I know why I was so curiously pleased that I had been hammered by a girl; not only was she a terrific ballplayer, but she was an avatar of a tidal shift in the culture. It used to be that basketball, and sport in general, was a male province, and now it isn't. I don't think we sing and celebrate that enough.

The Ballad of Jimmy Ward

Allow me the temerity of paraphrasing the late tart-tongued Mother Teresa: there are no great stories, only small stories told with great attentiveness. So I tell you a war story that has nothing to do with arrogance or fear or cash, the usual reasons we foment war. It has to do with a really lovely left-handed jump shot, the parabolic poem at the heart of the greatest of sports, the one invented in rural America long ago, our own wild sweet quicksilver tumultuous graceful gracious idiosyncratic characteristic basketball.

It's about a boy I'll call Jimmy Ward. He was the shooting guard for a basketball team here in the Wild West. Point guards came and went on that team, forwards shuffled in and out, centers lumbered and plodded and were replaced by other massive slabs of meat, but Jimmy was eternal, Jimmy played every minute, year after year, because Jimmy had the quickest, deadliest, loveliest jump shot anyone had ever seen, and even the most martinettish of coaches knew enough to leave him alone and let him happily terrorize defenses with his sharpshooting. He had divine range, and could drill that shot from anywhere; he was cat-quick, and could get his shot off against the grimmest of defenders; and he had exquisite judgment and timing—he never took a bad shot, was liable to stunning hot streaks, and had the killer instinct granted to a few great players who understand exactly when a crucial score will utterly deflate an opponent.

College scholarship offers piled up on the dining-room table of his house; Jimmy remembers his father grinning as he riffled through the pile, reading the names of the colleges aloud in wonder, colleges who would pay handsomely to have his son as a student or ostensible student, colleges who wheedled and pleaded, colleges with names of ancient heft and glow. But Jimmy declined the glories of collegiate sport; he wanted to be a United States Marine, one of the few and the proud. He joined the Marines one day after he graduated from high school. Soon he was in a war. Soon after that he lost his left hand. Soon after the war he did enter college, this time on an academic scholarship. Eventually he became a teacher, a profession he enjoys today, a few miles from where he was the star of the basketball team. He coaches, too—the very littlest kids, on the theory, as he says, that if he can get them to run and pass and savor the looping geometry of the game, they'll have good basketball genetics when their bodies begin to rise toward the patient stars.

He can't shoot jumpers anymore, of course, not having a left hand, and while I watched him coaching the other day, smiling at the way he barked happily at the swirling minnows in his care, I wondered where his jump shot went. Is it in the blazing sand far away where his hand is buried? Is it only in the memories of aging men? What else is lost when we go to war? What trillions of other small wondrous gifts vanish when hands fire rifles instead of basketballs? What ways to war with each other have we not even imagined yet, ways that will reduce us still further? Are we ever going to grow up as a species and figure out how to find the country beyond violence? Are we ever going to stop saying one thing about violence and doing another? Are we ever going to really live like joy is glory and blood is a crime?

Jimmy says we should have sports tournaments to solve international disputes—Hey, sports is stylized war anyway, he says, why not take it to the logical conclusion, and have an epic conclusive Israeli-Palestinian soccer match, or a chess match between India and Pakistan for final possession of Kashmir? And why not have sporting punishments for criminals, like a competition between Osama bin Laden and Radovan Karadzic to see who can clean the most toilets of the families whose children they murdered? I mean, says Jimmy, why not have some fun instead of the usual murder, you know? Because wars are just lots of murders, he says. No one ever admits that in public, except the guys who used to be in wars, guys who got murder all over their hands and can't ever get it off again.

I'll end here, with Jimmy smiling at us, a lot of nothing where his left hand used to be. A small story, one guy, one hand, one war. But, you know, where *did* his jump shot go? And why?

Two on Two

Once upon a time, a long time ago, I rambled through thickets of brawny power forwards and quicksilver cocksure guards and rooted ancient centers, trying to slide smoothly to the hoop, trying to find space in the crowd to get off my shot, trying to maneuver at high speed with the ball around corners and hips and sudden angry elbows, the elbows of twenty years of men through grade school high school college the park the playground the men's league the noon league the summer league, men as high as the seven-foot center I met violently during a summer league game, men as able as the college and professional players I was hammered by on playgrounds, men as fierce as the fellow who once took off his sweats and laid his shotgun down by his cap before he trotted onto the court.

I got hurt, everyone does eventually, I got hurt enough to quit, back pains then back surgery then more surgeries, it was quit or walk, now I walk.

The game receded, fell away, a part of me sliding into the dark like a rocket stage no longer part of the mission.

Now I am married and here come my children: my lovely dark thoughtful daughter and then three years later suddenly my squirming twin electric sons and now my daughter is four and my sons are one each and yesterday my daughter and I played two on two against my sons on the lovely burnished oak floor of our dining room, the boys who just learned to walk staggering across the floor like drunken sailors and falling at the slightest touch, my daughter loud lanky in her orange socks sliding from place to place without benefit of a dribble but there is no referee only me on my knees, dribbling behind my back and trick-dribbling through the plump legs of the boys, their diapers sagging, my daughter shrieking with glee, the boys confused and excited, and I am weeping weeping weeping, in love with my perfect magic children, with the feel of the bright-red plastic tiny ball spinning in my hands, my arms at home in the old motions, even my head and shoulders snapping fakes on the boys, who laugh; I pick up a loose ball near the dining room table and shuffle so slowly so slowly on my knees toward the toy basket eight feet away, a mile, a hundred miles, my children brushing against my thighs and shoulders like dreams like birds; Joe staggers toward me, reaches for the ball, I wrap it around my back to my left hand which picks up rapid dribble, Joe loses balance and grabs my hair, Lily slides by suddenly and cuts Joe cleanly away, he takes a couple of hairs with him as he and Lily disappear in a tangle of limbs and laughs, a terrific moving pick, I would stop to admire it but here comes big Liam, lumbering along toward the ball as alluring and bright as the sun; crossover dribble back to my right hand, Liam drops like a stone, he spins on his bottom to stay with the play, I palm the ball, show fake, and lean into a short fall-away from four feet away, the ball hits the rim of the basket and bounces straight up in the air, Lily slides back into the picture and grabs my right hand but I lean east and with the left hand catch and slam the ball into the basket all in one motion,

and it bounces off a purple plastic duck and rolls away again under the table,

and I lie there on the floor as Joe pulls on my sock and Lily sits on my chest and Liam ever so gently so meticulously so daintily takes off my glasses,

and I am happier than I have ever been,

ever and ever, amen.

Rec League

Three years ago I volunteered to coach the grade school boys in the local rec league here in Oregon. I did so for the usual reason men coach, because none of the other fathers would do it, even though I begged and sniveled and pleaded, but they all backed away slowly, their mouths filled with creative excuses, and as one guy said to me it was my moral responsibility to coach the boys because not one but two of the boys were my sons, so there.

So I coached, so to speak, that first year, and then again last year because none of the other fathers would do it and I had a year's experience anyway, and again this year because, heck, I have always been the coach for as long as anyone can remember, and partly as a way to try to stay sane I have kept notes about certain adventures and misadventures, like the time I started practice by making them run laps and then got into an interesting discussion with a dad about grilling fish and forgot about the boys until one of them threw up after running thirty laps, or the many times my players have been so excited they shot at the wrong basket, or the time my point guard used such foul and reprehensible language to the referee that we had to call two time-outs in a row we were laughing so hard, or the time we won ten games in a row and then lost a squeaker and I found out that the other coach had secretly scouted our team for the previous two weeks, or the time our center told me he couldn't play because a girl he had a crush on was in the gym and she was making him all nervous and everything, could I maybe ask her to leave? or the time a crow hopped into the gym and everybody freaked out, or the time a player on another team got hit in the nose and burst into tears and walked out of the gym and walked home, or the time we only had four players but won the game anyway although I thought I was going to have to carry all four guys home after that, or the time a ref really and truly did swallow his whistle and the other ref had to take him to the hospital, or the time a player on another team put his cell phone in his jock and when a pass hit him amidships his phone rang, or how the first year I coached my guys were such rotten free-throw shooters that when one of the guys finally hit one halfway through the season we called time and everyone shook his hand, or the kid we had one year who could just *not* get the idea of dribbling the ball down pat and ran with it everywhere with his arm out like a running back fending off defenders, or the game we played one time that was as close to perfect as I think I will ever see on this wild sweet holy earth, my boys sprinting and cutting and whipping passes and driving to the hole and not taking wild shots and actually playing defense and hitting the boards in such vivacious creative energetic exuberant fashion that sometime during the second half I leaned back in my rickety folding chair in the echoing elementary-school gym and wanted to cry for reasons that remain murky to me.

There were other reasons to cry. One time I asked a boy if he had a basket at his house on which to practice his vague grasp of the idea of a layup and he said quietly there was a basket near all three of his houses, his mom's and his dad's and his grandma's where he lived. And there was a boy who had a black eye and bruises on his shoulders and he told me he fell down the stairs but when I asked him if his dad was coming to the game he winced. There was a boy whose mom and her new husband sat on one side of the gym and his dad and his new wife sat on the other and the son, a terrific ballplayer, never looked at either his mom or his dad but stared at me with fearsome eyes during timeouts. I could never bear to take him out of the game because it seemed to me that the game was the one place he was happy.

But mostly it's been hilarious and poignant. I have seen some of these boys grow more than a foot taller. I have spent hundreds of hours with them in all the elementary school gyms there are in our town. I have given speeches at the end of the season about their diligence and grace as I handed out tinny trophies that they love and will probably have all their lives. I have made them run and laugh, which are good things to do. They have made me listen to their horrendous thumping music which isn't as bad as I thought it would be. We have talked about politics and books and girls and burgers. They have brought me back into the bright redolent funk of gymnasiums and the cheerful tedium of practice and the quivering tension of games. They have brought me back to the sinuous quicksilver geometry of basketball, the most American of games, with its energy and violence and grace and joy and competitive drive, its swing and rhythm and music. They have trusted me and confided in me and wept as I knelt down and looked into their faces and did my best to calm them.

For a while they gave me the extraordinary gift of their company as they went from being goofy boys to lanky young men, and here at the end of the last season I'll ever coach, I find myself savoring every shred and shard of the thing I didn't want to do three years ago. I sit back on my rickety chair and watch them, and the curious thing is that while occasionally now there is a flash of real creativity and grace, the very thing that you watch games for, those moments when brains and bodies flow, it's the egregious mistakes that I will miss the most—the ludicrous shot, the hopeless pass, the hilariously bad defense, the brain-lock moments. There was one last Saturday, when a kid got the ball, a new kid, a gentle sweet soul who'd never played the game before in his life, and he was so excited to actually have the ball and a clear lane to the basket that he ran delightedly to the wrong basket and scored. Everyone cheered and laughed and shook his hand and he blushed and the game flew on ancient and relentless but I sat there shivering with joy.

The Falcons

Drove past the burger place on the other side of town today, and up from memory swam nine grinning boys aged nine, sprawled around the plastic tables, as their grinning coach, yours truly, gave brief entertaining speeches about each boy, and his progress over the basketball season, and his most boneheaded mistake of the year, and his best games, and his work ethic, if applicable, and his generosity, if applicable, and his total goofy silliness (uniformly applicable), and then I shook his hand in the old way of my youth, and not in some modern hip-hop manner despite the boys spending the whole season trying to get me to learn their many cool handshakes, and then I clapped him on his narrow eager sparrow shoulder, and looked him in the moony eye, and said quietly, so only he could hear, that I was honored and pleased to have been his coach, as the rest of the guys and their proud moms and dads and bored-to-mildly-interested siblings applauded, and then the moms photographed their sons with their coach, who looked like a rumpled badger, and then it was the next boy's turn.

I had resisted the idea that each boy should get a trophy at the end of the year, feeling that trophies were devalued when everyone gets one, and that maybe three trophies would be plenty of trophies, best player and most improved and best teammate, and the boys would just lose the trophies anyway, so why bother? But one of my twin sons (both of whom were on the team) pointed silently to my desk, on which stands a basketball trophy I earned when young, and also my lovely bride, a subtle soul, asked me to reconsider my stance during the last practice of the season, so I sat there, that last weeknight, watching my team, as they ran through their drills and razzed each other and scrimmaged and razzed each other, and I realized I very much wanted to give each boy some talisman of effort and achievement, some marker of his commitment and my regard; so I bought nine little tinny golden plastic statues, and had labels engraved with the year and the name of our team (The Falcons), and carried them into the burger place for the awards ceremony.

I thought it would be easy, handing out trophies and making wry remarks, but as each boy came and stood with me, proud and shy and happy, I found that I was near tears; each boy was so very himself, silly and earnest and peculiar, both child and incipient man, that I stumbled and stammered through my speeches. It was so very much the end of something—something I had loved dearly and deeply, and not even because I loved the game so, and loved trying to teach it like a sinuous language, a deft craft, a calculus of joy. Even now, years later, I cannot quite find the words for that seethe of emotions: affection, pride, concern, even a sort of silent desperate hope that they would grow straight and true, and not grow into snide jackasses, and not get snared by drugs and drink, and always somehow miraculously retain something of their open genuine unadorned burbling bumbling verve. They were nutty and grave, shy and loud, heedless innocents in some ways and wise beyond measure in others; some had four parents and some just one; two were so tightly wound that you could see it would take years for them to find a shred of their true best selves; one so often played the clown that I worried he would be trapped in his performance and play the fool all his life.

The last two trophies went to my sons, and I tried not to weep aloud, for now we were deep in the ocean of wild love, where everything I felt for the other boys was quintupled and then cubed; and then we were done. There were lots more photographs, and then each boy peeled off with his family, and we all went home, but I wonder, this morning, if any of those boys, now young men of twenty, remember when they were Falcons, remember the day their coach laughed and wept at once as he handed out trophies, remember they were once nine years old, children and incipient men, remember their coach bending down and saying very quietly *It was an honor and pleasure to be your coach, an honor and a pleasure I will never forget.*

Twenty

Years ago when I coached the eleven- and twelve-year-old boys in our city basketball league, I had a kid named Joey who was tall and broad and hapless and the sort of kid who spent every minute cutting up, and capering, and clowning, and playing the fool in hopes that the other guys would pay attention to him, which was his great dream, for then somehow he would have something like friends, which apparently he did not have in the rest of his life.

I knew nothing about his family, though no kith or kin ever appeared to cheer him on in the two years he played with us; he arrived for and left from games and practices alone, on his bicycle, wearing the same ancient sweatshirt whether it was hot or cold or wet; he wore the same battered sneakers for two years, until one of the other kids' dads gave him a pair of his own epic sneakers one night after practice; and while he was not the worst basketball player we had, he was pretty clearly the second-worst. During his first season I concentrated on getting him to run up and down the court successfully, which is harder than it seems; basketball is a game of fits and starts and sprints and sudden motion, and Joey just could not get the rhythm of it, for a while; he would stay back on defense even as his teammates sprinted away on offense, and he had an inveterate habit of handing the ball to the referee, whether or not the gift was appropriate. I think he was impressed with authoritative uniforms, and felt some inarticulate urge to offer a gesture of respect whenever he came into possession of the grail of the game.

But he improved, little by little, as did his coach, and after a while I realized that he actually was a quick and diligent study; if I gave him a certain task or responsibility, he would focus all his bubbling energy on that task until the final whistle. One game I asked him to concentrate only on setting picks, and he set momentous mountainous thundering picks the entire game. Another time I asked him to concentrate on boxing out the other team's rebounders, so that his own rebounders had more space in which to rebound, and he cleared out bodies wonderfully all the way to the whistle. One time I asked him to focus on tipping balls to his teammates; another time it was shooting only if he was close to the basket; a third time it was outlet passes, at which he was terrific, to my surprise; that game I remember fondly as a track meet, a fast-break clinic, a river of swift baskets.

By the close of his second season Joey was our starting center and, amazingly, quieter; he still performed steadily for his mates, but not so

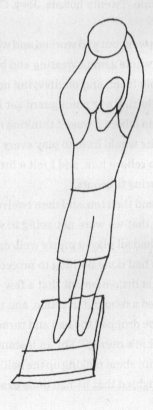

desperately as before; he still capered and mugged and mooned and hooted and clowned, but mostly now only at practice. We had a good season, and won our first two playoff games, before losing to the eventual champs in the final four, and it was during this last game that there was a moment with Joey I have always remembered. A few of the players noticed it, for which I loved them all the more, but none of the parents did; though I suppose each parent was naturally intent on their own child first, before catching up with the others.

I pulled Joey aside before the game and told him that his task this game was rebounding; the other team had three big guys and we had only him, and we needed boards to ignite our excellent fast break. I need twenty rebounds from you today, Joey, I said. You can do it. Just box out like a maniac, and use those quick hands, and whip that ball away to your cutters, and we will have fun. Don't worry about scoring. You just rebound like you and I know you can and we will be fine. Twenty boards, Joey. Can you get me twenty boards?

Yes, *sir*, he said, and he went out and worked and worked and worked and worked and worked the whole game, sweating and banging and grappling. I was intent on our whole team, and on divvying up minutes, and on the lazy referees, who were letting our point guard get hammered, and while I noticed Joey's herculean labors, I wasn't thinking much about him other than ruing the fact that he would have to play every minute for us to have a chance; I had no one to relieve him, and I felt a little bad about that, as I could see him sagging during timeouts.

We fell behind by six, and then ten, and then twelve, and with a few minutes to play it was clear that we were not going to win the game. I didn't feel too badly—my boys had all played pretty well, and my only regret was that the shoddy referees had done nothing to protect my exhausted point guard. But then came this little moment that a few of the boys and I saw and savored. Joey grabbed a rebound in traffic, and instead of turning and firing off an outlet pass, he dropped the ball and turned to me and shouted, "That's *twenty*, coach! That's *twenty!*" For an instant I was going to shout some coachish thing at him about picking up the ball!!, but he was so happy, and so proud, and so delighted that he had done exactly what I had asked him to do, that he just stood there beaming at me, as everyone else flowed away downhill toward the other basket. I think I will remember his shining face always. You never saw a happier prouder kid in your life. A minute later the game ended and I walked out onto the floor and shook Joey's hand and told him it had been a privilege to coach him for two years, which indeed it was, and still is.

Lefty

One summer when my son was at basketball day camp for a week at a time I would walk across campus and meet him for lunch. He was at the camp for a week. On Monday he was thrilled to see me and we ate our sandwiches together sitting in the bleachers. On Tuesday he was pleased to see me and we ate our sandwiches together. On Wednesday he smiled when I walked into the gym but he ate with the other guys. On Thursday he nodded to me when I caught his eye and then he went outside to eat with the other guys. On Friday I avoided lunch altogether but walked over to the gym in the afternoon and sat up in the bleachers watching the campers in their tournament games. The games were coached by the counselors, all of whom were or had been varsity players for the college. One coach had been a tiny burly point guard and his shoulders and arms and neck were totally covered with tattoos. Another coach had been a center and he was nearly seven feet tall and when he bent down to consult with his charges it was like a hemlock tree leaning down to chat with moss and lichen.

After a while a friend of mine wandered up from the floor and sat down companionably. He was the assistant coach for the college and he ran the camp and now that the final games were being played he had few moments off from supervision. We chatted about my son's virtues and vices as a ballplayer ("He's *evil* quick," said my friend, "and he never turns it over, but he needs a better outside shot, he needs to shoot more in general, and he has to learn to shift gears and stutter step and that sort of thing; he has to learn how to *confuse* bigger guys, you know?"), and then we watched the games for a while, as he picked out the tiny things that a master of the game sees and the casual fan does not, like particularly deft footwork, or how to quickly discern another player's weak points. He's a cheerful and gracious guy, and I was much enjoying his quiet running commentary, when he went quiet for a moment and then said Now *that* is cool.

What?

Far court, he said. See the tall kid in blue? Watch him for a few plays and tell me if you see it.

This kid was good—smooth, effortless, smart, generous; twice as I watched he created an open shot for himself and then paused a split second to let defenders come to him and then zipped the ball to a startled suddenly open teammate. A quietly excellent defender who'd just cut his man out of the play without drama. Boxed out well. Unhurried—that jumped out at me.

I mentioned all this to my friend who nodded and said Right you are. But here's your gift for today—look closely and you will see he's only using his right hand. He's a lefty. I watched him all week and he's left-handed. I think he doesn't want to dominate the game and he's playing righty to make it more competitive and he's hardly taken a shot. He's getting his teammates involved. Now that—*that* is cool.

We watched the end of that game and the lefty kid's team won by four points and his teammates were shouting and capering with delight. I watched carefully when the lefty kid shook hands with the other team and indeed he was a lefty. Then my friend and I watched my son's last camp game, in which he scored eight points, all on drives to the basket, and then my friend said he'd better get down to the floor for last speeches and stuff like that, and we shook hands, and I went back to work, but all the way back across campus I thought of the little generous tiny subtle gracious infinitesimal huge things that people do for their teammates of all sorts and stripes, and always have, and that cheered me up for the rest of the day, and for two whole days afterward.

A Note on Drills

I ceased to play the game I loved above all other games when I was about thirty, for vertebraic reasons, and for a long time afterward I thought that I was done with basketball, or more properly that basketball was done with me. But then sons were granted unto me, and they grew apace, and soon I was a basketball coach, first to my sons, and then to their fellow motley ruffians on our street, and then to their fellow criminals on the playground, and then finally to the fifth- and then sixth-grade recreational boys' basketball team in our winter city league.

These were two of the most exhausting and hilarious winters I ever spent, and still, ten years after I coached my last game (a loss by eight points, during which we got *robbed* by the refs, and the other team targeted our point guard for *constant* abuse, but who's bitter?) I wake up occasionally from a dream in which I have instructed the boys to run laps and forgotten to tell them to cease, and some of the boys, now in their twenties, are still doggedly circling the gym. My wife knows this dream well, and now when I snap awake moaning *Boys, enough!*, she hands me a little card that reads IT WAS A DREAM & IT'S YOUR TURN TO MAKE COFFEE, which it probably is.

Elsewhere I have written about many memorable moments from those two seasons, but this morning I would like to remember some of the peculiar drills I put the boys through, in an effort to get them to stop thinking of the game as a win-or-lose proposition, and more as a headlong adventure, a series of unrepeatable patterns, a miracle of meshed effort and creativity and imagination. It had occurred to me, within the first few minutes of our first practice, that their near-total ignorance of the game, which another man might see as a hindrance to be overcome or a problem to be solved, was actually a rare chance to teach them not just the fundamentals of the game, which any goober can learn by diligent repetition, but the deeply mysterious joy of the game when played well by several players at once. Talent, boys, I would often say, is vastly overrated, but generosity and imagination and slippery evil quickness are underrated, and it is the latter set of virtues that we are going to try to sharpen, especially as we seem minimally equipped with the former.

So we had the hot-potato drill, which entailed sprinting up and down while passing the ball instantly to a teammate; we had the touch-pass drill, by which I wanted them to get used to the idea that they didn't always have to catch a pass, but could just instantly redirect it to another sprinting elf; we had the river drill, during which they simply ran up and down in flowing weaving patterns, slowly learning that they could use their mobile teammates as screens and thickets and distractions for the easily duped defensive eye. We had the eye drill, during which I tried to train them to cut instantly away from the direction in which a defender glanced. We had the tip drill, by which I hoped to teach them that getting a hand on a loose ball was very often just as good as attaining possession of it. We had drills during which they learned to pass over their shoulders without looking, a drill that, I hoped, sharpened their sense of where their teammates were, or should be; although every time I think of that drill I see a manically energetic boy named Carl whipping the ball over his shoulder at supersonic speed game after game, and the ball either sailing untouched into the backcourt, or into the glower of parents in the stands, or hitting an unwary teammate right in the beaming pumpkin.

We had drills during which the boys did nothing but walk while spinning the ball on their fingers. We had a drill during which they had to stare at me while dribbling as fast as they could. We had a catch-and-shoot drill during which they competed to see who could get a shot off fastest. We had endless drills in which I tried to teach them to shoot layups and short jump shots with their left hands. We had drills during which they shot with their eyes closed, a drill by which I wanted them to learn to shoot unconsciously, with no worries about form. We had a drill called Coyote during which two players were freed from their normal defensive responsibilities to try to steal the ball anywhere it was. We even had a drill called Chaos, during which all five players on the court were freed to do whatever they wanted defensively, a scheme we unleashed occasionally when we were down by ten points or more. I dearly loved to loose Chaos upon an unsuspecting opponent, not because it ever worked very well, but because it was so hilarious to watch, as my boys went, briefly, bonkers; I am sure that there were games when the boys remembered nothing so clearly and so happily as the two minutes during which they were utterly free to cause conundrum and flummox as they liked. One boy, I remember, was so delighted when we went to Chaos that he would simply bound up and down where he was, with the most patent and infectious glee. Even now, after almost fifty years of playing and watching the game, I cannot remember that I ever saw anyone so deliriously happy on a basketball court, and I have seen players ecstatic after winning titles and hitting miraculous shots, and that sort of thing; but no one I ever saw was as happy as that boy, leaping in place as high as he could, over and over and over again, with a look of the purest joy you ever saw.

The Court Where My Sons
Used to Play Ball

Is only half a court, and it's tucked into a tiny verdant park between the library and the post office, in a dense shaggy old neighborhood, so that if you don't know where it is, you'll never find it, except by happy accident, which is how we found it one day when we were trundling to the library, and one son said *Hey dad hey a good hoop!*, which is a lovely line to hear.

We stopped and explored and indeed it was a perfect little beautiful half court, with one basket, slightly too high, with a double rim, which forces meticulous accuracy on a shooter; this pleased me for murky reasons. Also the court was lined with a thick laurel hedge on two sides, so that a loose ball could not rattle away into the street or the alley, and the other two sides opened onto the park, so a loose ball would just roll harmlessly into the grass, and the court wasn't pitted or puddled or mossy or littered with shattered glass and crumbled pebbled asphalt, and best of all there was no one on it, so my sons snagged the basketball we traveled with for just such emergencies, and they played there for an hour, that first day, as I sat in the park watching with complete and utter absorption.

There had been a time, when they were young, that I refereed their one-on-one tilts, partly as a representative of the loom of the law, and as stern defender of the sanctity of the game (no, you cannot double-dribble, or travel, or foul, even if you can get away with it, because that is not the way we play) but mostly as a chance to try to advise and applaud with muttered remarks from the hustings, but then I retired, as they entered their teen-agery, and watched happily as they got better and defter and more creative and confident—as they, in fact, got better than their father had been; which was, curiously and refreshingly, a deep and abiding pleasure; I had not known that a man's ego can be joyously washed away when his children do something better than he ever could.

But now and then many times after that first hour I watched as they spun and shot and hustled and dove, faked and hooked and blocked and boxed each other out, as they pulled up calmly from one or the other of the hedges and dropped long shots, as they baited each other into the slightly wrong move at exactly the right instant, as each grinned at a spectacular play by the other, and each hammered each other harder from affection and respect and annoyance and ambition; and then finally, when the game was over, I watched with a shiver as they gently touched fists, or brushed fingers, or just nodded in the ancient gesture that means *Thanks* and *Well-played* and *That was fun* and *Next time, brother, next time.*

But then they grew older, and drove themselves, and now when they go to play ball they say *See ya, Pop* at the door, and I watch as one flips the ball to the other as they fold into the car; and away they go, to one court or another, still playing one on one. I do not think they stop at that little court much anymore; but I did, yesterday, while trundling to the library, and I said hey to the laurel hedges, to the double-rimmed basket, to the mammoth cedar tree behind the basket, and I felt nine things at once, one of which was a tremendous gratitude to basketball, which is, among its many other subtle virtues, an extraordinary way to say *I love you.*

There Will Not Be So Many Chances
Left to Watch Us

The Coherent Mercy having given me two new sons at the same time, I vowed to do right by them and teach them basketball, so that they would be able to speak that joyful and creative and generous language, and battle each other happily and safely, and meet friends in the game, and learn to hone and focus their miraculous physical vessels, and always have a sport to come home to as meditation and refuge and release, in their hours of conundrum and confusion, of which, I knew too well, there would be many, such being the price of life;

And I did so. I gave them basketballs to putter around with when they were small, and took them to the park to shoot around as soon as they could hoist up shots, first with two hands and then with a wobbly one and then with a sure one, and I signed them up for leagues the instant they were eligible, and coached them myself for two years, at the ages when headlong begins to become heedful, in basketball and perhaps many other endeavors.

Then, in the way of things, they were on their own in the game, and to my great pleasure they both kept playing, played even more, played city league, played pickup and intramural ball at college, played constantly with their friends when they were home for breaks, played constantly against each other whenever they were home together, piling into the car laughing and coming home an hour later exhausted and exhilarated.

Now they are twenty-one, and yesterday they suggested that I should come watch them play, and for once I said yes. I have said no in recent years, remembering when their teenage games against each other dissolved into bickering, which I could not stand; but this time one son said quietly *There will not be so many chances left to watch us*, and he was right, and I was haunted by that line, so I went to watch them play. I stood in a little brick alcove at the elementary school as they got loose and then I watched with increasing amazement as they played one on one. They were much better than the last time I had seen them. One son, always a quick deft muscular athlete, now had the short jump shot and long set shot that he had not had last I watched. The other son, long and lean and limber, now knew his body, knew how to use his height down low, knew how to create space for an untouchable shot. And they knew each other; watching closely I could see one anticipate the other's spin, and get there first, or the other not bite on a beautiful show fake, but stay rooted and crowd the shot he knew would be launched away from the fake. They boxed each other out, they rebounded well, they hardly fouled, they gauged each other's angles and predilections and weariness with eerie intimacy. They hardly spoke, except to articulate the score. Hooks, jumpers, set shots, sidesteps, putbacks, fall-aways, reverses, teardrops, scoops, one driving layup with the off hand . . . I watched this all with such a tumult of emotions that I thrash for words. Pride, that they played cleanly and deftly, and they clearly and inarguably loved the game for themselves, as part of their own lives, part of their *own* pleasure. Appreciation, that they were *good*, they were fun to watch, they were good athletes but better ballplayers; and there is a difference between those things. A satisfaction or joy or shiver or rattle, that what I had so hoped for them, so dreamed might come true, *had* come true, that they were fluent in the language and harmony and melody and zest and narrative of the game. And, I suppose, somehow, in ways that I have been struggling to shape this morning, some deep tide of love. I love those boys in a million ways, those miraculous young men, those long muscled grinning no-longer-boys; and one of the deepest ways I love them was sung, yesterday, on a pebbled schoolyard court, with the basket an inch too high and the net a tick too tight, just before the rain.

Could It Possibly Be That Sport
Is More Than Sport?

Was talking to a slightly supercilious rugby player the other day who said, slightly superciliously, that *his* sport was the most honest and forthright of sports, because grim conflict is normal and natural as a reflection of the rough history of our species, and we have always been at war, and always *will* be at war, and a sport that is blunt and open about war is admirably unadorned, unlike other sports that decry contact, and mince around conflict, and create safe zones and sacrosanct buffers between and among opponents, such as volleyball and tennis with their intermediary nets, and baseball, in which the only guys you are allowed to crash into are your teammates by accident, and soon enough that will be banned, too, somehow, and soccer, in which the only time guys crash into each other is when they are *pretending* to do so, what an artsy and theatrical illusion soccer is, and track and swimming, in which opponents are not even walled off from each other by skinny nets, but by little cute precious bobbins, in swimming, and *lines painted in the dirt* in track, as if runners are little kids who cannot be trusted to run straight ahead, how insulting and degrading is *that*, I ask you?

He muddled on in this vein for a while, and I was listening idly, until he denigrated basketball as a noncontact sport, at which point I took the floor, and issued a fervid speech that went something like this: First of all, you woolly mammoth, I have seen and heard and experienced and survived some horrific collisions in basketball, and seen knees and ankles torn apart, and heard concussions happen, and broken fingers and wrists of my own, and broken the fingers of others, and of broken noses in basketball there is no end, but smashing people is not the *point* of basketball, as it is in rugby and football. Consciously and deliberately causing injury and mayhem is not rewarded in basketball; it is generally penalized, whereas in football it is celebrated and lauded, and the deliverer of pain and damage is applauded and saluted, as well as, in the upper reaches of said sports, slathered in money and hagiography, until such time as he leaves the sport, and soon thereafter finds himself drooling haplessly as he fills out insurance forms for his twentieth surgical procedure.

There *is* contact in basketball; one may, well within the rules, create and endure contact with another player; one may, at the edge of the rules, gently shove and physically impede another player; but you may not clock him, or try to shatter his teeth, or take a running head start and do your best to detach his cranium from his spine, because basketball is not a game of grim and ferocious violence, but of competing physical and mental creativity, in which leverage and angles and sleight of hand are the coin of the realm, and fakes and illusions and gear shifts and cheerful sneakiness are the lingua franca, and swift reactions and reflexes the quotidian fare. Do you have any idea what I am talking about under these words? Do you see what I am saying, that one game is indeed ancient and the other is futuristic, that one is rooted in who we were, and the other in what we might be? That one is predatory and the other is visionary? That one is naked battle with blood and meat and the other is stylized battle, battle pushed toward theater, battle as a spark to imagination, rather than battle as a reward in and of itself? That one sport is only mammalian, with all the awesome burl and muscle and fear and courage and camaraderie under duress that bands of hunters felt against cave bears, and the other takes the roar of our past and attempts to make it a new song for our species? Am I getting through to you at all? Could it possibly be the case, I ask, that sport is far more than sport, and is, much to our surprise and dawning pleasure, a riveting way to outwit war, to take that ancient unquenchable urge and bend it toward breathtaking and entertaining art? Could that possibly be? Sir?

A Language You Loved

One last note about basketball. A last testament, a final word. I think the sport is bigger than sport. I think it does say something about flow and creativity and liquid quickness and generosity and theater and joy more than any other sport on earth. I think it is a sort of language that sometimes is about competition and other times might be about theater, or summer, or friendship, or channeled war, or communal vibrancy, or refuge, or catharsis, or reinvention, or salvation, or lots of those things at once. I love that you do not have to be burly and tall and grim and muscular to be good and even great at basketball. I love that there is no armor necessary, no hiding of the face, no idiosyncratic equipment. I love that you can be bad at it but enjoy it immensely. I love that you can play it outdoors and indoors and on dirt and cement and asphalt and rubber and wood and even grass as I did once amazingly in Ireland. I love that it is a world sport now and people play it in maybe every country on earth. I love that it was invented in America. I love that no greedy international entity claims to own and supervise and manage the game. I wish we could use basketball tournaments to settle international conflicts. I love that the best referees are the ones who know how to manage a game without saying anything. I love how sociopathic behavior in basketball is penalized rather than rewarded as in football. I love how basketball players get to keep their teeth unlike hockey players. I love how basketball players are generally leery of steroids and such because in basketball getting bulkier is not actually a good thing. I love how the game has the same complex flavor with four or six or eight players as it does with ten; perhaps the game is even better with six or eight players than it is with the standard ten. I love how some countries have embraced the game with all their hearts and produced wonderful players seemingly out of thin air without a century of notable exemplars as we have in America. This seems promising to me and I expect to see superb players eventually from Nunavut and Nicaragua and Mongolia and Chad. I love how the game technically could go on forever and that it is theoretically possible to have a game with forty overtimes. I like that there are no such things as injury time or penalty boxes or headhunting or bounty payments in basketball. I like the blunt naked honesty of the game—we are going to try to score, and you are going to try to prevent us from scoring, and then we will reverse our ambitions, and after many turns each it should be fairly clear which team is more deft and creative and accurate and diligent than the other, at least for one game. I love the fact that the team you beat by twelve last week can very easily beat you by thirteen this week, for reasons that are often subtle indeed. I love that the game finally is about deft and swift and witty maneuvering of the remarkable physical machines that we were granted by a merciful providence; the game is about grace, dance, soaring, sleight of hand, entertaining subterfuge, vision, unselfishness. I love that lesser players can beat greater players by outwitting them. I love that even when you must stop playing the game because of injury or age, you can remain in and of and with the game by ratcheting up your attentiveness, so that you see things that you never noticed when you were there amid the whir and swirl of bodies, and now you realize slowly that you love it just as much, in a wholly different way, as you did when you were young and strong and swift and leaping and spinning and sprinting and as happy physically and emotionally and maybe even spiritually as you could be as a young wild mammal trying to sing a language you loved. I love that even though that was long ago it wasn't, not at all.

A Note of Thanks

Many of these essays and stories first appeared in *The American Scholar* magazine, in its electric version (https://theamericanscholar.org), and I thank Sudip Bose in particular, who edited me for three years with the lightest of hands. A gracious man. I must also thank the editors of *Notre Dame Magazine*, the *Christian Century*, the *Sun Magazine*, the *Kenyon Review*, *America: The Jesuit Review*, and *Eureka Street* in Australia (another very fine electric magazine, by the way, https://www.eurekastreet.com.au, and thanks especially to Tim Kroenert), in which others of these headlong inky adventures first saw the light of day, the swirl of ink, the fizz of an electric alphabet. Thanks too to the fine editor and writer Walter Biggins, who bravely took a shot at this book when it would have been so very easy to be cautious and reserved and leery, but he wasn't. And finally my awed thanks to the filmmaker Avery Rimer, who took the essay "His Last Game" and made an extraordinary loving wry pained bruised witty moving ten-minute film of it, which, I kid you not, was shown at the Cannes Film Festival. Unbelievable. I weep every time I see it and I watch it again every month. See www.hislastgame.com.